D0249889

# 9 THINGS THEY DIDN'T TEACH ME IN COLLEGE ABOUT

# CHiLDReN'S

## MINISTRY

Frank, Ryan, 1975—
9 things they didn't
teach me in college abou
c2011.

sa                08/31/11

HEY DIDN'T
TEACH ME IN COLLEGE ABOUT
CH🙂ILDREN'S
MINISTRY

RYAN FRANK

Standard®
PUBLISHING

Cincinnati, Ohio

Published by Standard Publishing, Cincinnati, Ohio
www.standardpub.com

Copyright © 2011 by Ryan Frank

All rights reserved. No part of this book may be reproduced in any form, except for brief quotations in reviews, without the written permission of the publisher.

Printed in: United States of America
Project editors: Lu Ann Nickelson, Elaina Meyers
Cover and interior design: MTWdesign
Typesetting: Dina Sorn at Ahhaa! Design

Unless otherwise indicated, all Scripture quotations are from The Holy Bible, English Standard Version® (ESV®), copyright © 2001 by Crossway, a publishing ministry of Good News Publishers. Used by permission. All rights reserved.

Scripture quotations marked (*NIV*) are taken from the *HOLY BIBLE, NEW INTERNATIONAL VERSION®. NIV®*. Copyright © 1973, 1978, 1984 by Biblica, Inc.™ Used by permission of Zondervan. All rights reserved.

Scripture quotations marked (*The Message*) are taken from *THE MESSAGE*. Copyright © by Eugene H. Peterson 1993, 1994, 1995, 1996, 2000, 2001, 2002. Used by permission of NavPress Publishing Group.

Facebook® is a registered trademark of Facebook, Inc., which is not affiliated with Standard Publishing. Starbucks® is a registered trademark of Starbucks U.S. Brands, LLC, which is not affiliated with Standard Publishing. PowerPoint® is a registered trademark of Microsoft® Corporation, which is not affiliated with Standard Publishing. iPhone® and iTunes® are registered trademarks of Apple® Inc., which is not affiliated with Standard Publishing.

ISBN 978-0-7847-2979-3

Library of Congress Cataloging-in-Publication Data

Frank, Ryan, 1975-
  9 things they didn't teach me in college about children's ministry / Ryan Frank.
    p. cm.
  Includes bibliographical references.
  ISBN 978-0-7847-2979-3
  1. Church work with children. I. Title. II. Title: Nine things they didn't teach me in college about children's ministry.
  BV639.C4F73 2011
  259'.22--dc22
                            2010034566

15 14 13 12 11 10   1 2 3 4 5 6 7 8 9

# CONTENTS

# INtRoDUCtIoN

The year was 1985, and I was ten years old. My dad gave me my first magic set consisting of a plastic ball and vase. The trick consisted of taking a small ball out of the vase and putting it in my pocket. When I said "Abracadabra!" the ball magically reappeared in the vase. I'm glad I started doing magic tricks as a kid because now it seems that I have to sometimes work "magic" in children's ministry. For instance, let me tell you what happened a few months ago on a Thursday night.

It was our church's annual missions conference, and a missionary was scheduled to teach the kids. Ten minutes before the start time, I asked the person in charge of the kids, "Is the missionary here?" She said he was running late and she gave me the look. You know, the look that screams, "What am I going to do? I need a super children's pastor!" I had to put something together—and fast! I sprinted to my office.

It had been a few years since the kids had seen the cross trick. (The cross trick is a powerful way to present the gospel to children, teens, and adults. Go to www.9thingsbook.com/crosstrick to learn more about it.) After snatching the cross trick from my office and running back to the classroom, the story of Nicodemus came to mind. So I had the cross trick and the story of Nicodemus. Now a creative opening was needed. Whipping into the church nursery, I grabbed a baby doll, diaper, and bottle. While starting upstairs, the thought hit me, *What if this isn't enough?* This meant running down two flights of stairs to the resource room and grabbing a few prizes for a last minute game. Are you tired yet? I was.

Making it back to the third floor with only three minutes to spare, I needed to get everything set up and do a rapid review of John 3. The kids were about to walk into the room and—you guessed it. The missionary showed up! I have to admit that I wasn't happy. Did he act remotely sorry? Nope. Did he apologize? Nope. Nevertheless, I showed grace and welcomed him with the best handshake I could muster.

The end of the story? Not quite. I filled a little tub with all the goodies for the lesson along with a small New Testament. I even scratched some of my thoughts on an index card and placed it in the tub. Now I have a ready-to-go lesson complete with all the stuff the next time I only have ten minutes' notice to teach.

Some things in life are learned best from experience. Because I've had lots of experience and learned a few things over the years, it only took ten minutes to put together a last-minute lesson. For example, I always think first of the hook because it can create wide-open eyes and dropped jaws. The hook can be a story, a special effect, or a good object lesson. That night it was the cross trick. Next, I choose a Bible story that goes with the hook and gather visuals, like the baby doll, diaper, and bottle. Experience is a great teacher.

Back up a few years to 1992. I was only sixteen. My pastor approached me and said, "We need someone to teach junior church. Will you try it on Sunday?" I tried it and loved it! That's what started me on the career path of children's ministry. I went on to major in Christian Education at Indiana Wesleyan University and had some terrific professors and classes. The "Working with Children" class taught by Keith Springer was great because he has a very practical, hands-on approach to ministry. I still use many of his ideas, and he invites me to join his class each year to talk about children's ministry.

I greatly appreciated my college education, but, as a new children's pastor, I still had a lot to learn. No one coached me how to handle moms and nursery workers who don't get along. No one taught me that the church bulletin is the absolute worst place to recruit volunteers. No one helped me understand that my job description might change over time, such as shifting from being the children's pastor to the pastor who partners with parents in raising spiritual champions.

In this book I'll share nine things they didn't teach me in college about children's ministry. Whether you're brand new to children's ministry or have been at it for years, whether you're a Sunday school teacher or a vocational children's pastor, I'm confident that you'll learn from my experiences and the experiences of others—both the successes and the big flops. Let's get started!

# DEDICATION

**To my wife Beth**
You are my best friend and life partner.
Your love for God and others is contagious.

**To our daughters Luci and Londyn**
We pray that you will know, love, and serve
Jesus Christ every day of your lives.

# AcKNowLeDgemeNts

I want to thank my coworkers and friends whose encouragement and support helped bring this book into being:

- o the staff at KidzMatter Ministries,
- o friends and church staff at Liberty Baptist Church,
- o and all the great people at Standard Publishing including my editor and friend, Lu Ann Nickelson.

I also want to thank my wonderful wife, Beth, who shares my passion for ministry. While her name may not appear on the cover, her fingerprints are throughout this book. She is my primary source of inspiration and support. I love you!

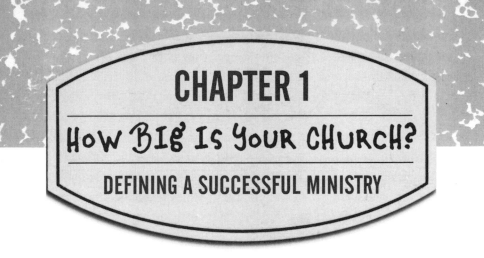

# CHAPTER 1

## HOW BIG IS YOUR CHURCH?

### DEFINING A SUCCESSFUL MINISTRY

In more ways than one I've always looked up to my dad—he's six feet eleven inches tall! His height helped him set some serious records in his basketball career. It's also nice to have a really tall person around when we need a Goliath in kids' church. As nice as it is to have a dad with some height, at the end of the day it's not all that it's cracked up to be.

Some things that we value in life really don't matter. A person's height is one. Size isn't everything.

People always ask me, "How big is the church where you serve?" Asking about the size of my church is like asking how tall I am. What difference does it make? Remember, size isn't everything. People may ask this question because they equate success with size. A church of twenty thousand must be more successful than a church of five thousand. A church of five thousand must be more successful than a church of two hundred. Really?

What defines success in the church? What about success in children's ministry? Is it big numbers? An expensively-themed environment? A high-tech check-in system? There's nothing wrong with those things but they don't measure success—at least not in God's eyes.

In the heart of every leader is the desire to succeed. But how do you do it? In this chapter we'll stick close to the Bible. I'm sure you're not interested in my definition of success and, no offense, but I'm not all that interested in yours. Let's see what God has to say about it. Agreed?

In the New Testament, Paul has a lot to say about ministry. Nothing fired him up like the work of the church and lives being changed through Jesus Christ. Let's look at his letter to the church in Rome.

*"First, I thank my God through Jesus Christ for all of you, because your faith is being reported all over the world. God, whom I serve with my whole heart in preaching the gospel of his Son, is my witness how constantly I remember you in my prayers at all times; . . . I long to see you so that I may impart to you some spiritual gift to make you strong—that is, that you and I may be mutually encouraged by each other's faith. I do not want you to be unaware, brothers, that I planned many times to come to you . . . in order that I might have a harvest among you, just as I have had among the other Gentiles. I am obligated both to Greeks and non-Greeks, both to the wise and the foolish. That is why I am so eager to preach the gospel also to you who are at Rome. I am not ashamed of the gospel."* (Romans 1:8-16, *NIV*).

Let's drill deeper into this passage and look at six building blocks for successful ministry in God's eyes.

# success starts with the Right perspective

*"I thank my God through Jesus Christ for all of you"* (Romans 1:8, *NIV*).

When was the last time you paused to thank God for the privilege of serving children and their families? It's easy to forget the many blessings of children's ministry.

## YOU GET TO SHARE THE GOSPEL WITH KIDS

If you want to reach the largest hidden mission field in the world, look down! The probability of five- to twelve-year-old children accepting Christ as Savior is 32 percent. That number drops to 4 percent between the ages of thirteen and eighteen. It creeps up slightly to 6 percent for adults.[1]

Lilly Conforti is the Children's Ministries Director at the Full Gospel Church in Island Park, New York. When she heard these statistics, Lilly said, "It gives me an added reason to keep on preparing lessons, loving kids, and pouring God's Word into little lives. Jesus saw the value in kids! I am blessed to serve the children in our congregation."[2]

> If you want to reach the largest hidden mission field in the world, look down!

## YOU GET TO IMPACT THE WORLDVIEW OF CHILDREN

A worldview is the way a person sees the world and answers the big questions of life. A Barna Group research survey shows that "a person's worldview is primarily shaped and is firmly in place by the time someone reaches the age of thirteen."[3]

## YOU GET TO PARTNER WITH PARENTS

Parents are ultimately responsible for the spiritual development of their children and you can champion them in this great cause.

## YOU GET TO BE LOVED AND SERVE IN A MINISTRY THAT'S JUST PLAIN FUN

In the heart of every person is a desire to be loved by someone. In children's ministry, you can be loved by a bunch of little someones! In *Toy Story 2,* Buzz Lightyear said to Woody, "Somewhere in that pad of stuffing is a toy who taught me that life's only worth living if you're being loved by a kid."[4] How true is that?

Plus, you don't have to wear a choir robe or police teenagers. You get to play crazy games, sing exciting songs, and plan fun events. You also get to help the Bible come to life for kids while building life-long relationships—and that's just the beginning!

## SUCCESS BUILDS ON GOD'S WORD

*"Your faith is being reported all over the world"* (Romans 1:8, *NIV*).

Wherever Paul went, people were talking about what God was doing at the church in Rome because people there were being changed to become like

Jesus. This was before TV, the Internet, and cell phones. Paul wasn't following the Romans on Twitter or getting text messages from the deacons in Rome. But people were being changed and the word was spreading like wild fire.

The million-dollar question in children's ministry leadership is not about a program, model, or leadership style. It's this: are kids being changed to become like Jesus?

Stop reading for just a moment and get a fresh reminder that God is at work. You are still reading! Seriously, stop and think about it. God wants to work today just as he did in Paul's day.

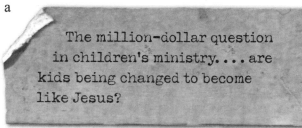

The million-dollar question in children's ministry. . . . are kids being changed to become like Jesus?

He wants to show up (big time) in your ministry.

How does God work? The primary method is found in the next verse. God chooses to work through people "preaching the gospel of his Son" (Romans 1:9, *NIV*).

Never replace the centrality of God's Word in children's ministry. It's in the context of God's Word that lives are changed. Early in my ministry I asked one of the workers how he felt kid's church was going. This gray-haired man with a big heart for kids looked at me and said, "Ryan, you're doing a great job. But if you're going to skip something on the schedule, never skip the lesson!" Sounds like simple, common sense advice, but not a week goes by that I don't remember those words.

## FIFTEEN WAYS TO PRAY FOR THE KIDS IN YOUR MINISTRY

Pray
- that God will give you a love for each child.
- that they will come to know Christ as Savior.
- that they will love God with all of their hearts.
- for their parents and families.
- that they will choose the right kind of friends.
- for spiritual stability during tough times.
- for the needs of their hearts that you may not know about.
- for protection in their lives.
- that they will have wisdom and discernment.
- that they will love God's Word.
- that they will learn to pray.
- that they will have concern for others.
- that they will have integrity in all areas of their lives.
- that they will have courage to do what's right.
- that they will look for ways to serve the Lord.

# SUCCESS HINGES ON PRAYER

*"How constantly I remember you in my prayers at all times"* (Romans 1:9, 10, *NIV*).

Your best intentions in children's ministry are not good enough. You'll accomplish very little without God's help. I'm not talking about tangibles, like a record-setting VBS or a new facility, but those eternally important intangibles such as children knowing, loving, and serving Jesus. Only God has the power to ensure that the enemy stays away and that the children in your church will walk with him.

There's a volunteer on our children's ministry team who knows the power of prayer. Recently, while praying with him, my heart was warmed and tears swelled in my eyes as he prayed for at least one hundred kids by name. This man knew how to pray and it got my attention. (I believe it got someone else's attention too!)

# Success Takes Love

*"I long to see you so that I may impart to you some spiritual gift to make you strong"* (Romans 1:11, *NIV*).

One mark of great leaders is a growing capacity to love people. Can you pick up on the love in Paul's words? Look at this passage from *The Message* Bible: "The longer this waiting goes on, the deeper the ache. I so want to be there to deliver God's gift in person and watch you grow stronger right before my eyes" (Romans 1:11)!

Why are you in children's ministry? If you're looking for a pat on the back, you're headed for disappointment. Almost every week someone tells my pastor about his great sermon. I want to stick my finger in my throat and barf (only kidding). It isn't fair! The kids never tell me how great my lesson was. They never thank me for bringing the Scriptures to life. Here's the thing: it's okay because I didn't sign up for a pat on the back. I signed up because I love and care about kids and their families.

In 2 Corinthians 12:15, Paul says, "I will most gladly spend and be spent for your souls." Now that's love! Paul was willing to give everything he had, including his life, to lead people to Jesus. Paul knew that a successful ministry takes love.

Gladys Aylward was born in London in 1902.[5] She had a desire to serve as a missionary but the China Inland Missionary Society said she wasn't qualified. However, this was one determined girl. Her opportunity came in the person of an aging missionary, Mrs. Jeannie Lawson, who was looking for a young assistant to carry on her work. Gladys saved up her money and, in 1930, spent her life savings on a train ride to Yuncheng,

Shanxi Province, China, where she ministered in a remote area.

In 1938, Japanese forces invaded her village. Gladys single-handedly led over one hundred orphaned children to safety. She was forced to lead them on foot on a one-hundred-mile trip over the mountains to the safer province of Sian. On the journey, she became sick. She collapsed when they finally arrived at Sian. The doctors were amazed that she made it as far as she did—she was suffering from typhus, pneumonia, a relapsing fever, and malnutrition.

Gladys is a hero, especially to those of us who love and serve kids. She sacrificially loved those children and cared about their souls. She is an example of what God can accomplish using the least of us.

Every act of love makes a difference, even in the lives of children and people you may never meet. Dr. Wess Stafford says, "Your small pebble in the pond of one child's life may send out ripples that eventually transform many others."[6] Never forget the importance of each small pebble of love!

> Continue to do your best because you're under obligation to God and to those kids and families whom you're serving. Don't quit!

## SUCCESS REQUIRES COMMITMENT

*"I am obligated"* (Romans 1:14, *NIV*).

Paul went on to communicate the commitment he had to the ministry. Paul wasn't in ministry for personal reasons or because someone asked him to fill a slot. He served because of a sense of obligation. I challenge you to tell God that you're a "lifer" in children's ministry until he lets you know otherwise.

There are times when children's ministry is rewarding. It's great when a child says that she can't wait to come back next Sunday or a child tells you that he wants to ask Jesus to be his Savior.

However, there are other times when the ministry isn't as rewarding and the kids aren't as receptive (you all know what I'm talking about). On those days, continue to do your best because you're under obligation to God and to those kids and families whom you're serving. Don't quit! Say it with me: I am not going to quit! (Seriously, say it out loud right now!) May God give you the grace to say these words and mean them!

This level of commitment flows from an intimate relationship with God whom you serve. Keep your relationship with the Lord first in your life and the commitment part will come much easier.

# Success Centers on the Gospel

"I am not ashamed of the gospel" (Romans 1:16, NIV).

Methodology and programs change, but God's measurement of success never changes. Sometimes we look for creative, innovative, dynamic, exciting ways to succeed while overlooking the obvious. Want to know what's really important to God? The gospel!

If the gospel is so important, we need to make sure we understand what it is. Let's go to Jesus and hear what he has to say. "The thief comes only to steal and kill and destroy. I came that they may have life and have it abundantly" (John 10:10). The gospel is the message of Christ (his death, burial, and resurrection) and the abundant life that he offers.

Success is not found in programs. There's nothing wrong with sporting events, family-oriented services, and concerts, but good programs don't define success.

Success is not found in environments. To be successful you don't have to cough up thousands of dollars to make your building look like a theme park. There's nothing wrong with themed environments, but there are more important things than paint and plasma screens.

> Although success is not found in themed environments, there's nothing wrong with them! Visit www.9thingsbook.com/ environments to see photos of some creative environments.

Success is not found in the latest and greatest stuff. Success doesn't automatically come from having a high-ticket check-in system or a brand new playground.

Success is not found in the size of a ministry. We'll never reach a generation by pointing to the size of our church or being proud about what we've done.

Programs. Environments. Stuff. Size. These are all good but they don't indicate success.

Success in God's eyes is found in being faithful. Faithfully proclaiming the gospel week after week—that's success. Helping kids enjoy the abundant life that God offers—that's success.

HELLO
my name is

Beth   Evan   Greg   Rick
    Nathan   Clayton   Kyle
Nicki   Glen   Erick   Tyler

# Talking with Facebook Friends

**How do you measure success in children's ministry?** Here is how some of my Facebook friends answered this question.

"Being able to rejoice with parents when their child reaches those spiritual milestones—salvation, baptism, learning to memorize Scripture." Beth Plank

"The kids must be able to answer two questions: 'Did you have fun?' and, 'What did you learn?'" Nathan Pearce

"To measure success in your children's ministry, look no further than your mirror. Kids are taught by example. If you, the children's minister, demonstrate a passionate intimacy with Jesus, the kids you minister to will follow." Evan Tyler Reid

"If and when I encounter them as adults of any age serving our Savior, and when, one day, I hear Him say, 'Well done.'" Rick Glover

"When you look around your kids' church and see kids passionate about serving God and excited to bring their friends to church. When kids come to a saving knowledge of Jesus Christ and are living out that faith till He comes." Greg Ferguson

"When they realize that God has a big plan for their lives, and become 'doers' of the Word." Kyle Hayes

"Are you duplicating yourself in a consistently growing team of leaders who love kids as much as you and desire to see them live their lives for Christ?" Clayton Poland

"If I can look around and see children and their families following Jesus Christ with me as a result of my obedience to God, then that is an early indicator of ministry fruitfulness. If they become disciple-makers themselves (especially independent of my direct influence), then that is further confirmation. In the final analysis, however, God will be the judge." Glen Woods

"Am I being obedient to what God has called me to do? If yes, then I have succeeded." Nicki Straza

"Not by numbers or accolades, but by stories of kids and families who are growing closer to God and one another." Erick Ashley

"When parents see life changes in their kids, and when you see life changes in your volunteers." Tyler Thompson

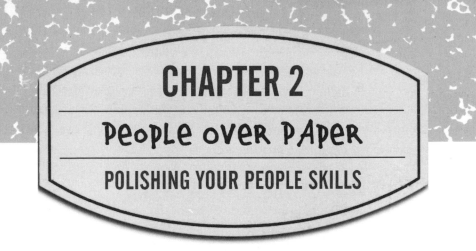

# CHAPTER 2

## People over Paper

### POLISHING YOUR PEOPLE SKILLS

Jesus' ministry was all about people. He spent thirty-three years showing us how to build a relationship with God and how to build relationships with others. But sometimes we forget that ministry is about people! Ever gone home on Sunday thinking how great ministry would be if it weren't for people? I have. Here's the deal—no matter how you slice it, ministry is ALL about people.

Your ministry will only be as successful as your ability to relate to others. I have found that a majority of people who fail in ministry do so for this reason—they don't relate well to others. Underline this next sentence: People work is more important than paperwork! At the end of the day, any program that you come up with will only be as effective as you are at building relationships with people.

Jesus set the example for us. Remember the woman at the well? Jesus connected with her one-on-one. When the woman went into town, she told everyone, "A man just told me everything I've ever done!" How's that for connecting with someone? In case you're thinking, *Of course he could do that—he's the Son of God,* remember that Jesus came to set an example for us. We should be equally committed to building relationships with people.

Your ministry will shine when you polish your people skills. It starts by taking a look inside your own heart. You'll never put people over paper until you are willing to be a servant.

## Develop A Servant's Attitude

It's time to get an attitude—the attitude of Jesus, that is. Developing proper people skills starts with having the attitude of a servant. Look at what Jesus said:

> *"Whoever would be great among you must be your servant, and whoever would be first among you must be your slave, even as the Son of Man came not to be served but to serve, and to give his life as a ransom for many"* (Matthew 20:26-28).

Jesus served others. Do you? Too many leaders are concerned about getting attention and credit instead of being a servant. I am learning that God's kingdom will grow if you don't care who gets the credit.

Jesus washed dirty feet to demonstrate this principle. A lot of children's ministry is about foot washing. It's about putting away pride and serving others just like Jesus. Every time you change a diaper, clean up vomit on the carpet, or are the last one to leave the church, you demonstrate servanthood. Philippians 2:5 says, "Have this mind among yourselves, which is yours

Stop and do an attitude check. Do you have the attitude of a servant or is it all about you?

in Christ Jesus." Stop and do an attitude check. Do you have the attitude of a servant or is it all about you? If the latter is true, you'll be miserable and so will the people around you.

# UNDERStAND People's NeeDs

Once you get your attitude in line (that takes work) you need to understand some things about the needs of the people you serve. In reality, needs haven't changed much since Adam and Eve. Methods and programs change, but the needs of people haven't. Listed here are eight basic needs of people. As you read this list, think about the volunteers in your children's ministry.

## EVERYONE NEEDS TO BE LOVED

It's been said that if the devil can't make you bad, he'll make you busy. Normally when we get busy the first things to get sidelined are our relationships. Some of us are too busy to love people like we should. Sometimes the greatest thing we can do for people is to love them.

How do you love others? You follow the example of Jesus. He put the needs of others before his own—ultimately he gave his life!

Loving others doesn't mean that you turn all warm and fuzzy. Trust me, I am not a warm and fuzzy guy. Emotions wear off with time. Loving those you serve is not something you feel, it's something you choose to do. When it's all said and done, the thing that matters most is making a choice to put others first. People will forget that amazing VBS program or the hours you spent learning how to juggle four toddlers in your arms while pouring Kool-Aid. However, they won't forget the love you showed them.

> When it's all said and done, the thing that matters most is making a choice to put others first.

## EVERYONE NEEDS TO BE NEEDED

One of my all-time favorite TV series was *24*. The star of the show, Jack Bauer, was a guy who needed to be needed. When there was a threat to national security, the President knew whom to call. Jack would put it all on the line when there was a need.

Jack Bauer isn't the only person who needs to be needed. Everyone does. One of your biggest tasks is recruiting people—right? Recruiting starts by letting people know about the needs in your ministry. There are people who would love to get involved but they have to know the needs and they need to be asked—personally asked. Some people just won't be comfortable approaching you. Too often we wait for people to come and talk to us, or we ask the same people who are already too busy.

9 THINGS THEY DIDN'T TEACH ME IN COLLEGE ABOUT CHILDREN'S MINISTRY

## EVERYONE NEEDS COMMUNITY

You've probably heard the old African proverb (thanks in part to Hillary Clinton) that says, "It takes a village to raise a child." The idea behind the proverb is that kids need a community along with a family. Here's the thing: kids aren't the only ones who need a community.

Community is tough to find in our mobile society. We live in a world where Facebook and Twitter become substitutes for long-term, personal communities. It's too easy to be high-tech but low-touch in today's world. People need to experience life with others. Paul described the church as a body, not each person as a body, but each person as a part of the body. "If one part suffers, every part suffers with it; if one part is honored, every part rejoices with it. Now you are the body of Christ, and each one of you is a part of it" (1 Corinthians 12:26, 27, *NIV*).

Communities are created when Christians lock arms and serve God together. Some of my best friends are people I serve with in the church. We have different backgrounds, different professions, and different stories. However, serving God in children's ministry is the common denominator that ties us together.

## EVERYONE NEEDS TO BE UNDERSTOOD

How well do you know and understand the people you serve with? I'm not asking if you know how many student books they get each quarter. Do you understand their pains and problems?

Remember the woman caught in the act of adultery as recorded in John 8? The religious leaders reminded Jesus that the law said she should be stoned. Jesus then wrote in the dirt. (It bugs me that we don't know what

Jesus wrote. That might be one of my first questions when I get to Heaven.) Jesus then said, "If any one of you is without sin, let him be the first to throw a stone at her" (John 8:7, *NIV*). One by one they walked away.

Think about what was going on in that woman's heart and the emotional trauma she was experiencing. She was no doubt embarrassed and afraid. Her life was laid out in front of the community. She could have been stoned to death. When her accusers walked away, Jesus said, "Then neither do I condemn you. Go now and leave your life of sin" (John 8:11, *NIV*). That's the kind of understanding heart that every minister needs!

How do you get to know and understand the people in your ministry? Here are a few pointers to get you going.

1. Be friendly. Get in the habit of smiling and saying a happy hello to everyone in your ministry. If you are a task-oriented person like I am, you will find yourself running around the church on a mission and bypassing the people you rely on the most—your volunteers. Stop running. Start smiling. Be genuine.

2. Learn the art of small talk. Get to know your volunteers on a personal basis. Work on it one small conversation at a time. The people in your ministry want to know you and they want you to know them.

3. Lighten up. Some of you don't have this problem but some of you might. Don't be so serious and intense that people are uncomfortable around you. Lighten up a little. You'll find yourself surrounded by people.

4. Ask others for help. People love to be asked their opinion, so go out of your way to ask questions like, "What do you think about

this new curriculum?" or, "How do you think we should handle the problem we had with the boys in kids' church last Sunday?" Then once they talk, sincerely listen and thank them for their ideas.

5. Support with prayer. When someone tells you about a problem, take thirty seconds and pray right then and there. I like to call these thirty-second prayers. I've had many thirty-second prayers in my tenure as a children's pastor. These prayers take place in the church foyer, in the back of the kids' church room, on the sidewalk at the church, or at the gas pump. Small prayers help you understand people.

## EVERYONE NEEDS ENCOURAGEMENT

Christians should be the greatest encouragers. Encouragement is to a team what wind is to the sails of a sailboat—it moves people forward. Consider the amount of criticism many people endure at work, school, or even at home. Think about canceling out those words of criticism with words of praise and encouragement. Be a cheerleader for those serving in children's ministry. (Although I refuse to wear a short skirt and carry pom-poms.)

Cheering on your team can start with simple notes of encouragement. They go a long way. You can e-mail someone, but I suggest turning off the computer and sending something in the mail. After all, it's nice to go to the mailbox and find something other than a bill now and then. I see your head nodding.

Here's an example. Send a card to a volunteer you noticed really going above and beyond in her Sunday school class. What does it take to make that person's day? Two minutes? Forty-four cents? The cost of postage may change but the needs of people don't.

For several years I've sent a note of encouragement to a different person every day of the week. It has become a habit in my life. It's one of the best uses of my time I can think of.

Some churches do annual appreciation events for their children's ministry team members. One church literally rolled out the red carpet for their volunteers and invited me to speak. The theme was "A Night with the Stars." There was valet parking and the paparazzi even showed up with their cameras.

"We had Mardi Gras Night," says Larry Shallenberger from Grace Baptist Church in Erie, Pennsylvania, about a recent large event he planned for his church's volunteers. "I went online to find out what the colors for Mardi Gras meant, and I learned they originally were chosen to reflect the royalty and power of God. I utilized those colors, ordered Mardi Gras decorations, and went all out decorating. We had Cajun food, and to take advantage of the teaching moment of the Mardi Gras colors, we asked our volunteers to form groups and think of ways they saw God's power, faithfulness, or wealth in their teaching ministries over the past year."[7]

When you create an environment where people are encouraged, you aren't going to have a problem with volunteers quitting because you won't be able to drive them off with a stick!

> For several years I've sent a note of encouragement to a different person every day of the week.

## EVERYONE NEEDS TO FEEL IMPORTANT

If you want more volunteers, make heroes of the ones you've got. Since you're reading this book, I have to believe that you understand the importance of children's ministry. However, not everyone in the church feels the same way you do. To many people, children's ministry is simply babysitting. Because of the lack of encouragement within some churches for people who work with kids, volunteers can be very lonely and feel unappreciated.

Effective leaders do everything possible to make volunteers feel valued and appreciated.

## EVERYONE NEEDS TO BE PART OF SOMETHING SIGNIFICANT

Many children's ministries rotate teachers in and out like a revolving door. Be careful of that because it's easy for volunteers to develop a "slot filling" mentality. Go ahead and make the big "ask." (See more about that

## WAYS TO MAKE HEROES OF YOUR VOLUNTEERS

- Communicate appreciation from the pulpit.
- Host an annual appreciation event.
- Deliver notes, candy, and other surprises to them before class begins.
- Tell volunteers that you're praying for them.
- Recognize volunteers in the church bulletin or newsletter.
- Have a volunteer of the month and post the names on a plaque.
- Invite volunteers and their families to your home for dessert.
- Give service awards.
- Send notes of encouragement.
- Ask members of the congregation to adopt a volunteer and pray for the volunteer every day.
- Send your volunteers to training events.
- Remember their birthdays.
- Stop running down the hall and speak a meaningful "thank you!"

in chapter 5.) Ask people to make a big commitment versus filling slots. People want to be a part of something significant. If volunteers are only filling slots, they're probably not making a big difference.

How well are you communicating that your volunteers are part of something hugely important? If you have a vision for your ministry, re-member that God gave that vision to you. Don't get frustrated when your volunteers don't automatically understand it. God didn't give the vision to them—he gave it to you, remember? It's your job to communicate it to them and let them see how important it really is.

The best way I have found to do this is by sharing success stories with volunteers. When a child comes to trust Christ as Savior, don't keep it to yourself! When a new family with children joins the church, share the good news! When you get a new volunteer, let everyone know about it! This can be accomplished in printed memos, e-mails, the church bulletin, on giant posters, and even one-on-one.

## EVERYONE NEEDS PRAYER

It's easier to say, "I'll pray for you," than it is to do it. When a teacher calls and says she won't make it to church because her child has a high fever, ask to pray with her right then. When you're in a personality conflict with someone, the last thing you want to do is pray for that person, but it's the first thing you need to do.

Remember—you don't have to have a thirty-minute block of time to pray. Take advantage of small pockets of time to pray, like when you're driving down the road (don't close your eyes, please) or waiting for an ap-pointment. Prayer makes a difference.

# INvest ToDAy

A statement comes in the mail every month about my retirement funds. I don't understand everything on that statement. But I do understand this: I'd better invest today or in the future I'll wish I had. The best place for you to invest time and energy is in the people in your ministry. The payoff is huge and you'll be glad you did.

## Interview with Jim Wideman
### Children's Ministry Specialist and Associate Pastor
World Outreach Center, Murfreesboro, Tennessee

**Ryan Frank (RF):** Do most children's pastors have a hard time getting along with grown-ups?

**Jim Wideman (JW):** Most children's pastors are more comfortable relating to kids than with adults. We must be able to communicate with children but we must also be able to talk with parents and volunteers. Most of the calls I get from children's pastors concerning adults are questions on how to deal with workers and other staff members. If you cannot lead and impact adults you'll never have an outstanding ministry to children.

**RF:** We joke in our office about how much brother Jim likes lists. If I asked you for a list of tips for dealing with adult volunteers and coworkers, could you give me twelve?

**JW:** Yeah, buddy. Here you go.

1. Realize you need help.
2. Let people get to know you as a leader and as a real person.
3. Be personable.
4. Be a good leader (set the example for others to follow).
5. Explain the hows and whys as well as the whats. Be a teacher.
6. Admit when you're wrong. Take responsibility for your mistakes.

7. Always side with authority.

8. Use your MBWA (manage by walking around) degree.

9. Dare to confront.

10. Say thank you. The more of this the better.

11. Solicit ideas and opinions from others.

12. Look for ways to help others look good.

You asked me for twelve, but I'm going to give you five more.

13. Be an encourager.

14. Don't be a time stealer. Respect the time of others.

15. Serve those over you.

16. Dare to communicate. Keep others in the know.

17. Don't guess or assume if you don't know.

**RF:** Do you have one word of advice for people who want to improve their people skills?

**JW:** The choice is all yours. Only you can make the choice to be as effective with adults as you are with kids!

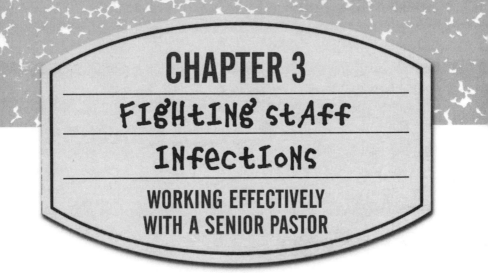

# CHAPTER 3
## FiGHtiNG stAff iNfectioNs
### WORKING EFFECTIVELY WITH A SENIOR PASTOR

Do you ever wish you could vote your senior pastor off the island? (If you're in the same building as he is when you're reading this and you can't shout out loud, you may want to shout out a big YES in your head.) Guess what? At some point he has probably wished the same thing about you.

A staph infection is a bacterial infection that grows deep below the skin. This kind of bacteria usually enters the skin through open cuts and can be life threatening. This chapter is not about staph infections, but "staff" infections. Staff infections grow deep too, entering through the mind and going right to the heart. They threaten your personal life and ministry and must be avoided at any cost. Go ahead and pat yourself on the back for reading these pages— you're on the right path.

Father-in-law. Pastor. Boss. Those words describe my senior pastor.

I joke with people and say that this brings job security! After all, I'm married to his oldest daughter and am the father of his grandchildren! Working with and for your father-in-law really can be a great thing. For that matter, every relationship between a children's pastor and senior pastor can and should be great.

Some of you may report to someone besides the senior pastor—that's okay. The principles in this chapter still apply to you. Some of you serve as children's pastors or directors of children's ministries on a volunteer basis. You're not officially on staff and receive no paycheck. For those in this category—way to go! Because you probably either report to the senior pastor or other staff member officially or unofficially, I hope you'll keep reading.

# start THRIVING

Here's the chapter in eighteen words: you will never be effective in ministry until you stop surviving and start thriving with your senior pastor. In the next few pages I'll share twelve tips for helping this happen. Are you ready to start? Let's dive in.

## 1. MAKE COMMUNICATION A PRIORITY

I have a great relationship with my senior pastor but it has been work. Hard work. One big reason it has been hard work is because we are polar opposites. He's people-oriented; I'm task-oriented. He likes to think; I like to do. I've learned the hard way that making communication important is critical in our relationship.

Communication must be a priority. Do your best to communicate with your senior pastor every way you can. Copy (or bcc) him on important e-mails. Give him a copy of everything you print for children's ministry. When something good happens, make sure he knows. When there are problems, make sure you tell him about it before someone else does.

> When something good happens, make sure he knows. When there are problems, make sure you tell him about it before someone else does.

While you want to make communication a priority, don't barrage him with minute-by-minute updates. Remember, he's a busy man. But the moment you hear about "trouble in River City," let him know. Senior pastors don't like to be surprised.

"It's important to find out what kind of communication your pastor wants," says Janice Dickey, children's pastor at Faith Family Church in North Canton, Ohio. "Mine likes a weekly report with details of class numbers, volunteer numbers, salvations, etc. It also has spread sheets attached that show year-to-date numbers. Some pastors want more detail and some do not. My pastor likes short and concise information."[8]

## 2. FAN THE FLAME

Stay in tune with your senior pastor's vision for the church. Discover his vision and be sold out to it. It's not easy to keep in tune with his vision when you're with the kids a good part of the time, so do whatever it takes to keep a pulse on his vision. Every week I go online to listen to my pastor's sermon because I want his vision to transfer to my heart.

Start fanning the flame of your pastor's vision. The best way to start is by sitting down with your pastor and expressing your desire to support his vision. This takes time together. By spending time with him, you will get to know how he feels and thinks. It will make it easier to support and promote the vision that God has given him.

Here's a little secret I've learned as a children's pastor. When you support your pastor's vision, he will support yours. Together you can be an amazing force in the kingdom of God.

## 3. MAKE YOUR PASTOR SHINE

One of the best tips for fighting staff infection is to go above and beyond for your pastor. When he needs some creative help, go overboard. If he asks you to organize an event, do everything in your power to make it the best event ever.

Look for areas where your pastor is weak and ask him how you can help. Good assistants are committed to making the leader succeed. When he wins, you win.

When my pastor wanted to start blogging, I jumped at the chance to help him set up his blog and taught him how to use it. When he wanted to start sharing his sermons online, I worked hard and made it happen. These are practical ways that I was able to help him and make him shine.

Remember that you belong to a team. It's not all about you and your ministry with children and families.

## 4. BE SOLUTION FOCUSED

Problems and ministry go hand-in-hand. When problems come knocking on your door, there's nothing wrong with getting help from your pastor.

Working together through problems is a smart move. However, avoid talking to him about a problem unless you have some possible solutions. Your pastor has enough on his plate. Before you talk to him, have some ideas that you can put on the table.

Unfortunately when some senior pastors see their children's pastor coming, they only see someone who needs more—more help, more square footage, more toys, or more money. Instead of asking for more stuff all the time, why not offer to buy your pastor lunch and paint a picture of the children's ministry you're dreaming about?

> Why not offer to buy your pastor lunch and paint a picture of the children's ministry you're dreaming about?

Show him how your solutions will be a big win for the entire church. Solution-focused conversations will win the attention of your pastor.

## 5. DON'T HAVE TUNNEL VISION

Tunnel vision is a medical condition that results in a loss of peripheral vision. As a result, a person with tunnel vision can only see objects within a circular field. Tunnel vision can happen in your ministry too. It occurs when you lose the vision of the ministry of the entire church and only see your ministry.

One thing your pastor has that you don't have is perspective. He knows the pulse of the people and what's going on in every ministry. If you push for that budget increase, that major project, or that big calendar item because you have tunnel vision and only see your ministry, you're going to build walls between you and your pastor. Tear down those walls by being a team player.

Andy Ervin is the children's and family pastor at Salem Fields Community Church in Fredericksburg, Virginia. He understands the danger of tunnel vision and shared with me about cross-pollination in ministry. "Recently in a team meeting we had a discussion about cross-pollination. This is when ministry leaders/departments/areas speak into other areas besides their own. Each ministry benefits from this because the collaboration turns into productive ministry experiences. It keeps philosophy and ideas flowing because we all care about each other's area of ministry. People are hesitant at first but as trust grows so will the bloom of effective ministry."[9]

## 6. BE FLEXIBLE

As an assistant to your pastor (this is who you are, you know) anything can be your job. Be flexible. Several years ago when our church needed a college pastor, I didn't say, "I only do kids." More money or perks weren't offered, but I served as college pastor for a year and a half while continuing to serve as children's pastor. When our church needed a bus director, I didn't say, "I don't do oil changes." I'm still the bus director. It's not my favorite job, but serving the needs of our church comes first. (I delegate the oil changes, in case you wondered.)

I hope you're always willing to do whatever is needed. Whether it's cleaning the restrooms, locking up the church building, or making sure the oil is changed on the church bus—be flexible! It's a great way to fight staff infections.

If you are a senior pastor reading this, please empower your children's pastor to do what needs done! Avoid the gopher factor. The gopher factor occurs when the children's pastor's job description is reduced to tasks such as folding mailers, fundraising, hosting guests, and general "I don't have time to do this so you do it for me" sort of jobs rather than ministering to kids and families. Your children's pastor needs to be flexible but also needs to be empowered to do his or her job with your full support.

## 7. LISTEN BETWEEN THE LINES

Effective assistants learn to listen between the lines. Sometimes your senior pastor will try to tell or ask you something without coming right out and saying it. For example, a few weeks ago my pastor asked if I wanted to make a hospital visit with him. Normally I would be cool with this, but the hospital was an hour away and I was swamped. When I asked if he really wanted me to go, he replied, "If you want to. We could talk about stuff on the way there." To make a long story short, I listened between the lines and went with him.

One more suggestion—honor your pastor's preferences. There are a lot of Sunday mornings when my choice would be to leave the tie in the closet. My pastor has never told me that wearing a tie on Sundays is mandatory, but I know it's his preference, so I honor it. When you listen between the lines that deadly staff infection will lose out.

## 8. HELP YOUR PASTOR IN PRACTICAL WAYS

Directors of children's ministries are busy. Sometimes they think they are the busiest people in the church. News flash—they aren't. Pause and take a look at your pastor's schedule. My pastor is one busy guy. He prepares three to four sermons a week, meets with everyone from the church staff to new members, visits people at home and the hospital, and makes short and long-term plans for the church. He has a personal life on top of all that.

Look for practical ways that you can help your pastor. It might be getting his car washed before a funeral or making a hospital visit for him if he is crazy busy. You might think that sounds like kissing up, but it's not. It's treating him like you want to be treated. Looking for practical things you can do to help your pastor will go miles in fighting staff infections.

## 9. BIBLICALLY RESPOND TO CORRECTION

I struggled with this one for years and still do. It's tough to take correction but it's imperative if you're going to thrive as a team.

Early in ministry I really struggled with negative feedback from the pastor and others in the church. My defenses would go up and I would take it way too personally. During one of those early years in ministry I went over the children's ministry annual budget—way over. The pastor pulled me into his office and lovingly reprimanded me. Without going into details, just know this: I didn't respond biblically. I got mad and ended up having to apologize a few days later.

It took me a few years to learn that just because my actions are being corrected or a question is being raised, my character is not being questioned. Big difference.

## 10. SPEAK UP

Bill Hybels, senior pastor of Willow Creek Community Church in Chicago, was asked by *Today's Children's Ministry*, "What communication do you like to regularly receive from your children's ministry?" Here's what he said: "An information loop is very important. At least one time a week, I'd suggest writing a personal note to the senior pastor telling him about some good thing going on in children's ministry. 'We've added another volunteer this week and thought you'd want to know and rejoice with us.' Or, 'Had a kid pray for the first time in 4th grade—first time he ever prayed out loud. Just wanted you to know that there probably is a family celebrating this.' Maybe try, 'Just want you to know that I think you do a great job and I'm proud to be on your staff.' And definitely, 'You'll never know how grateful we were for your mention of children's ministry this weekend.' Authentic affirmation and encouragement go a long way."[10]

Senior pastors don't always get the full picture of what's happening in children's ministry. Sometimes they only hear about the problems. No one knows the great stories like you do, so when you hear them, be sure to pass them on.

I make an effort every week to ask volunteers to tell me their stories of how their Sunday went and how the kids responded. This is another way to let your volunteers know that you care and it gives you more stories to pass on to the pastor. Stories are good for people because they provide inspiration and motivation.

## 11. GUARD YOUR INTEGRITY

When talking with senior pastors, the one thing they're always looking for in assistant pastors is people they can trust. If your pastor can't trust you, you have big problems. Trust is the number one quality your pastor needs from you. This doesn't come overnight. It has to be earned.

Do what you say you'll do. See projects through to the end. Never talk behind your pastor's back. Be loyal. Own your mistakes. Never lie or cover up a mistake.

Pastors never expect perfection, but they do need staff members they can trust.

## 12. PRAY FOR YOUR SENIOR PASTOR

Whatever you do, don't forget to pray for your senior pastor. Here's a way to pray for your pastor, especially if you have trouble remembering what to pray about. Use the letters of the word "pastor" to remind you of specific prayer requests.[11]

P—Purity. Pray that your pastor will remain pure in the face of constant pressure in an immoral culture.

A—Adversity. Pray that your pastor will confront adversity with faith and endurance.

S—Strength. Most pastors work long hours and at least six days a week. Pray that he has the strength to continue his ministry.

T—Teaching. Pray that his teaching and preaching will be effective, powerful, and clear.

O—Organization. Your pastor has more to do than any one person can handle. Pray that he will prioritize correctly.

R—Rest. Your pastor needs rest. Pray that he will sleep well each night and that he will take enough time away from ministry so that he does not get worn out.

Let your pastor know that you support him and are praying for him. You'll be glad you did.

Go to www.9thingsbook.com/31 to download a free thirty-one days of prayer for your pastor calendar.

# Infection Free

You will only be successful in ministry when you learn to form a partnership with your senior pastor. Exodus 18 tells about the time when Moses learned that he couldn't work alone, but needed a team. Get your senior pastor on your team and be on his team. Amazing things will happen when you're staff infection free. You might even get a birthday card from him next year.

HELLO
my name is

Tina  Angie  Steve  Susan
Dorothy  Johanna  Judy
Jennifer  Ben  Cindy  Brian

# Talking with Facebook Friends

**What is one word of advice for having a great relationship with your senior pastor?** Here is how some of my Facebook friends answered this question.

"Serve your pastor in all things, at all times. Always do your best to make him look good. Help him by putting your best foot forward." Steve Spencer

"Express praise in public, express concerns in private." Susan Payne Hughes

"Talk and communicate often, openly, and honestly. Don't let him hear about an issue in your department from someone else." Dorothy Whipp

"Affirm him and show your appreciation and communicate good news about the children's department often." Johanna Townsend

"Communicate to him what's going on in your ministry and also in your life! You need to be able to share life together in order to have more than a working relationship. Ministry goes deeper than the day-to-day activities of the church." Jennifer Yee

"Respect: It's his vision God has given him. Follow that vision for the church and align children's ministry to that vision." Cindy Christensen Fiala

"Golf, lots of golf!" Ben Kesselring

"Respect and honor in front of others. Fun staff meetings behind closed doors."
Angie Lingle Roberts

"Marry him." Tina Houser

"Marry his daughter and treat her like a queen." Judy Frank (my mom)

"Trust!" Brian Ebersold

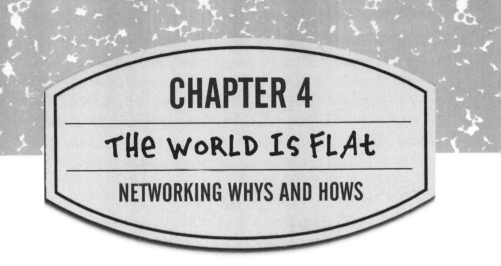

# CHAPTER 4

## THe WORLD IS FLAt

### NETWORKING WHYS AND HOWS

It's easier today than ever to reach around the world and network with others. In 2005, Thomas Friedman wrote a groundbreaking book about global connectedness entitled *The World Is Flat: A Brief History of the Twenty-first Century*.[12] Phones and Facebook, blogs and widgets, Twitter and texting have changed the way we connect.

More people are online and connected today than ever before. According to Internet World Stats, 1.8 billion people globally are Internet users.[13]

When I was in college and the topic of networking came up, there were three options. First, you could jump on an airplane and shell out a wad of dough for a conference. Second, you could get in your car and drive to a networking lunch—that is, if you were lucky enough to have a network in your area and your car would make it. Third, you could pick up the telephone and call someone.

There will always be a place for face-to-face networking. Years ago I was struggling with thoughts like, *Are people looking down on me because I'm the children's pastor? Am I missing out on a bigger and better ministry because I'm back with the kids?* It took a workshop leader named Mike Bright from Standard Publishing to help put those lies behind me. He helped me recognize that those were lies of the enemy to keep me from doing what God wanted me to do. I left that conference with a new resolve!

## A WeB of ReLAtIoNSHIPS

Networking is an interconnected system of things or people for a purpose. We're interested in the people part. I like to think of networking as developing a web of relationships that makes everyone better.

Some people in ministry neglect the web—not the World Wide Web, but the web of relationships. They don't prioritize it and often claim they don't have time. However, relationships are essential to those serving in ministry.

After graduating from college in 1998 and joining a church staff, two things happened. First, the big bucks of four hundred dollars a week started rolling in. Second, I thought I knew everything there was to know and that we had the be-all, end-all children's ministry. That was a bunch of bologna. I didn't know everything—and still don't, and I needed other people—and still do!

## CoNNectINg PoINts fRoM the BIBLe

The familiar passage from Hebrews 10:24, 25 is usually used when talking about church attendance and fellowship, but there's also an application for connecting with Christians on a larger level.

*"And let us consider how to stir up one another to love and good works, not neglecting to meet together, as is the habit of some, but encouraging one another, and all the more as you see the Day drawing near"* (Hebrews 10:24, 25).

What are some of the good things that happen when we're connected with others? A small section in one chapter of a book would never be enough room to cover them all, but let's think about a few things from this passage of Scripture.

## CONNECTING POINT 1: NETWORKING HELPS ME LOVE OTHERS
*"Stir up one another to love"* (Hebrews 10:24).

Some people in the church are good at stirring things up—and it's usually trouble! God wants Christians to stir each other up to love! This is a big benefit of networking with others. You may feel unloved, unappreciated, and all alone. But get around other people who love God and kids like you do and you'll realize these three things aren't true.

Networking not only gives others a chance to show you love, but it also gives you opportunities to love others. Some of you reading this book may feel like you can't stir up anyone to love because you have nothing to give—you're burned out. It can seem at times that those of us in ministry are the most unloved and unappreciated people in the world. Agree? We are often criticized, questioned, and attacked. That's why connecting is so important. When someone you've connected with is having a bad day or feeling burned out, you can speak or even tweet (more on that later) words of love and encouragement to that person. And someone will probably do the same for you.

## CONNECTING POINT 2: NETWORKING IMPROVES MY WORK
*"Stir up one another to . . . good works"* (Hebrews 10:24).

Get out the spoon again! Christians aren't just to stir up one another to love, but also to good works. When something is being stirred, it's constantly moving. Do you ever feel like your ministry is going nowhere and something needs to change? One of the best ways to keep the creative juices moving in your ministry is by networking with others. Here's what I mean:

o Networking keeps you current in the world of children's ministry. You can stay in the know about people, curriculum, events, and ways to recruit and train volunteers.

o It accelerates professional development. This is why I choose to *attend* one conference every year—no speaking, meetings, or book table. I just attend. Networking makes me a better leader.

o Networking gets conversations rolling. You can discuss hot topics, talk about great service projects for kids, and develop new strategies for partnering with parents.

o It's a way to pour into others. Networking is only as valuable as the amount of effort you want to put into it. Bag the "what's in it for me" mentality. People get turned off when it's all about you. Look for opportunities to bless others.

## CONNECTING POINT 3: NETWORKING BRINGS ENCOURAGEMENT
*"Encouraging one another"* (Hebrews 10:25).

The devil, according to legend, once advertised his tools for sale at a public auction. When the prospective buyers assembled, there was one oddly-shaped tool which was labeled "Not for sale." Asked to explain why this was, the devil answered, "I can spare my other tools, but I cannot spare this one. It is the most useful implement that I have. It is called Discouragement, and with it I can work my way into hearts otherwise inaccessible. When I get this tool into a man's heart, the way is open to plant anything there I may desire."

Children's pastors have one thing in common. No, it's not the fact that church janitors seldom speak to us. It's that we're all subject to discouragement. Paul knew what it was like to be discouraged. That's why he surrounded himself with good friends in ministry like Silas and Timothy.

Go to www.9thingsbook.com/conferences for a list of some great children's ministry conferences you can attend. ☺

When feeling discouraged and needing a lift, I've learned to pick up the phone and call a friend. I need doses of encouragement to keep me going and growing.

## CONNECTING POINT 4: NETWORKING PREPARES ME FOR THE BIG DAY
*"All the more as you see the Day drawing near"* (Hebrews 10:25).

The writer of Hebrews says that there couldn't be a better time to

- Find someone to teach for you so you can go to the adult worship service again.
- Hang around friends who love God and want to help you in your spiritual life.
- Find a prayer partner.
- Attend a conference or retreat.
- Attend an adult Sunday school class or small group.

start connecting, especially as the return of Jesus comes closer and closer. *The Message* calls it "the big Day." I love that! We don't know when the day of Jesus' return will be, though many signs seem to be coming into alignment. The important thing is to be found faithful when he returns. Connecting with like-minded believers will help you be ready.

One of the biggest dangers of being a children's pastor is that you can grow disconnected spiritually. You are so busy working for God that you forget about your relationship with him. Especially in children's ministry, you find yourself "back with the kids" and out of fellowship and worship with other adults. Don't be a lone ranger. Be committed to engaging with others in your own spiritual development.

## CoNNectiNg oNLiNe

The world is flat. Have I said that yet? It's easier today than ever before to engage with others in ministry. It's easy to connect! Anyone with access to the Internet can join in on this networking thing. Let's think about three ways to connect online.

### TWITTER

Since its creation in 2006, people as diverse as President Obama to Britney

Spears are on Twitter. Recently my wife Beth and I took Luci, our oldest daughter, to visit her great-grandparents. When we walked into the house, we heard MC Hammer on TV being interviewed about Twitter. We weren't in the door ten seconds before Grandpa asked, "What's Twitter?" It's fun explaining it to someone who's pushing eighty.

Twitter is a free social networking and micro-blogging service. No, I didn't use those terms to explain it to Grandpa. Here's what I said. Instead of sending a dozen e-mails or text messages, you send one message to your Twitter account and it goes to all your friends. It's like a giant bulletin board where anyone can stick a short note.

If you're not using Twitter to network, here are a few reasons to give it a try:

o Twitter allows you to meet new people. I know—a little obvious. Unlike Facebook, you don't have to be accepted as a friend to start communicating. A simple "follow" is enough.

o Twitter is simple. It does one small thing and does it well. Twitter lets you share what's happening now. In one hundred forty characters or less you can keep up with others and let them know what you're doing. I've heard it all, from "Staff meeting in full swing" to "My favorite musical instrument is the ice cream truck."

o Twitter gives instant feedback. Got a question about curriculum? Ask. Need a new game for Wednesday night? Ask. Looking for a place to eat the next time you swing through my hometown of Converse, Indiana? I doubt it.

o Twitter is a creative way to learn from each other. I joined Twitter to hear what others had to say. Every now and then I get invited to a Tweetup—a real-time meeting organized on Twitter.

o It makes you think about your life. Asking yourself, *What am I doing?* and *What can I share with others?* several times a day is a good exercise. It keeps me intentional about how I choose to spend my time.

If you're not a Twitter user, check it out. If you don't like it, you can always do something crazy like actually talk to people in person.

Go to http://twitter.com/r_frank to follow me on Twitter!

## FACEBOOK

Facebook started as a social community for college students. Now people of all ages around the world are on Facebook. It's a ginormous online community. Here are some tips for getting the most out of Facebook for networking purposes:

o Make your profile public. You can make your profile private or public to people who aren't your friends. If you're interested in networking, make it easy for people to find you by going public with your profile.

o Use a real photo of yourself. Don't hide behind that goofy Facebook profile icon. You want people to find you so you can connect. Don't use your baby picture or a picture of your pet canary.

- Ask questions. Having trouble calculating how many fish crackers the average three-year-old can inhale in five minutes? Post a question and give people a chance to answer. The answer—forty-two(ish)!
- Show an interest in others. Take a few minutes and let people know that you care about what's happening in their lives. Be careful about posting comments on every single thing that any particular person says, especially if the person is of the opposite sex. Your good intentions may be misunderstood.
- Write on the wall. I know, I know. You yell at the kids at church when they do this and here I am telling you to do it. It's okay on Facebook. Your wall is where you talk to your friends and they talk to you. You need to actually write something every now and then and let people know you're alive.
- Join groups related to your ministry interests. There are groups on Facebook for just about everything, such as "How Headphones Get Tangled Up on Their Own, I'll Never Understand" (182,362 members) and "For Those Who Have Ever 'Pushed' A Pull Door" (186,715 members). There are also quite a few for children's ministry. Do some searching and you'll be amazed.

## CMCONNECT

Want the inside scoop on a social networking site like Facebook that was created by a children's pastor for those involved in children's ministry? It's CMConnect. Michael Chanley launched the site in June 2008. The site has grown like wildfire with over six thousand members at the time of this writing.

Stop reading for a few minutes, jump on a computer, and go to www. cmconnect.org. It has a lot to offer! Here are a few tips:

o Sign up for a free account and get your profile set up. Now's the chance to talk about all the great things happening in your life. Got some pictures? A screamin' funny video from camp last summer? A great song you wrote? Start sharing.

o Find a group and get plugged in. Just like Facebook, there are a ton of great groups to join. Groups are the place to go to get some serious conversations going. You can even start groups of your own.

o Jump into the forum discussions. See the sidebar for just a sampling of the discussions.

## CMCONNECT FORUM DISCUSSIONS

- What do your kids do at the beginning of kids' church?
- What book would you recommend for a parenting small group?
- Has anyone tried a family VBS?
- What do you call a group for fifth and sixth graders?
- Do you have Sunday night activities for three- to five-year-olds?

These are just a few of the many discussions you'll find. Remember that networking is a two-way street. It's only as effective as your willingness to participate.

Spread the word! Invite your friends in ministry and volunteers in the church to join the site. It's free, easy, and only takes a few minutes. They'll thank you for it.

# WHeN It's ALL SAID AND DoNe

Networking with others in ministry may be one of the most important skills you can develop. My daughter Luci's favorite ride at a large theme park is the boat ride where hundreds of figures are dressed like children of the world singing the song, "It's a Small World."

> Networking with others in ministry may be one of the most important skills you can develop.

In light of this chapter about networking, let's rewrite the lyrics of the song. Sing repeatedly an excessively insane number of times until it's permanently etched into your brain.

It's a flat world after all.
It's a flat world after all.
It's a flat world after all.
It's a flat, flat world.

It is a flat world and that's why it's never been easier to connect. Before the close of each week, ask yourself: With whom did I connect this week to expand my network? Whom did I encourage? With whom did I share some creative ideas?

# Interview with Gina McClain
## Director of Children's Ministries
Faith Promise Church
Knoxville, Tennessee

**RF:** Gina, what are the main reasons you use social networking?

**GM:** Ideas and encouragement. When I need ideas, I can throw out a question and gain immediate responses from a diverse group of people trying to accomplish the same thing I am—leading kids to love Jesus. The encouragement piece is key. But that tends to be more indirect. I gain encouragement from hundreds of tweets every weekend as people celebrate things happening in their ministries.

**RF:** What online tools do you use to connect with others and what do you like about each one?

**GM:** I can be pretty fickle when it comes to online tools. I've tried Google Wave, Facebook groups, and CMConnect groups. Each of these comes with its own benefits for collaboration. But the tools I use consistently are Twitter and Facebook. When I want to hear about some of the biggest challenges facing children's ministers, CMConnect is a great tool. For personal connections in ministry, e-mail is the system that works best for me. Call me old-fashioned, but e-mail still works.

**RF:** I love reading your blog, www.ginamcclain.com. How has your blog enhanced your ministry?

**GM:** It's crazy how the blog has morphed. Originally I started the blog when I was on staff at LifeChurch.tv because I found that parents in the church didn't know me well. Their view of me was based on ninety-second interactions we shared on the weekends.

My blogging shifted when I found that my readers consisted of more than parents. In fact, the majority were children's ministers or volunteers at other churches. These readers were hungry for thoughts and ideas that challenged the way they did ministry. We all share a common desire for learning and a need to challenge and sharpen each other.

The thing I love most about the blogs I read is their diversity. They range from highly techie and innovative, challenging me in the tools I utilize to grab kids' attention, to deeply theological, leading me to closely examine what I teach kids. God uses each of them to shape how I do ministry.

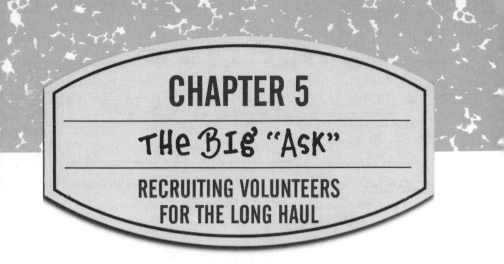

# CHAPTER 5

## THE BIG "ASK"

### RECRUITING VOLUNTEERS FOR THE LONG HAUL

On www.kidzmatter.com, I recently asked this question: What are the three biggest issues facing your children's ministry? Here's what several hundred children's ministers said:

#1: I don't have enough volunteers.
#2: I have little or no budget.
#3: Other activities take priority over church involvement.

You're probably not surprised that a shortage of volunteers is number one. Ask those you know in children's ministry about their biggest challenges. Recruiting and keeping volunteers will usually surface to the top.

If you're an avid *K! Magazine* reader (I hope so!) you're going to think that children's ministry expert Jim Wideman wrote the next few lines. Jim loves talking about Jethro and Moses. One day Jethro pulled his son-in-law, Moses, into his office (probably a tent) and told him he needed to recruit some volunteers—and fast! With this new force of volunteers, Moses could focus on the urgent spiritual needs of the people while the volunteers worked on less critical things. Thousands of years later, volunteers are still needed to do the Lord's work (minus the tents and camels, of course).

Children's ministry requires more volunteers than most other ministries. Too often, though, we beg for volunteers and will take anyone who can fog a mirror. How do you recruit volunteers who will last for the long haul? Recruiting volunteers for ministry is a lot like recruiting players for a baseball team. Here's what I mean.

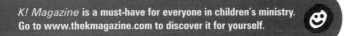

*K! Magazine* **is a must-have for everyone in children's ministry. Go to www.thekmagazine.com to discover it for yourself.**

# It stARts wItH A CoACH

Having a team of awesome volunteers starts with a coach—that's you. People line up to play for a great coach. In junior high I had a basketball coach who was a jerk. Strong words, but it's the truth. He was mean and there was no other way around it. Some of us quit the team a few weeks into practice. You see, no one wants to play for a lousy coach.

Put on your cap and do everything you can to be an excellent coach. Excellent leaders attract excellent people approximately 100 percent of the time. Commit to excellence. One of the best ways to do this is to learn from other leaders. Follow them on Twitter. Hang out with them. Read their books and blogs. Listen to their podcasts. Do whatever it takes.

# IDENTIFY THE POSITIONS

Identify the open positions in your children's ministry. Every baseball coach knows the positions he needs to fill and so should you. Let me give you an example:

Corey and Andrea approach you after church and share that God has laid it on their hearts to serve together in children's ministry. The last thing you want to say to them is, "I'm not sure if we need help." Big mistake. You have to strike while the iron is hot. If every teaching position is filled, isn't there always a need for prayer partners, substitute leaders, or someone to organize the cabinets or resource room?

Once you identify the positions, it's worth your time to develop ministry descriptions for all of the positions. Then you can e-mail or give the descriptions to interested people. This does a couple things.

## IT GIVES THE QUALIFICATIONS

Having ministry descriptions shows exactly what's needed and what the qualifications are for the different ministry positions. In baseball, the requirements to be a pitcher are known. That's why a batboy knows he isn't ready to pitch. In children's ministry, there might be someone who would be a great organizer but isn't ready to teach. Ministry descriptions help people get into the right positions and not get frustrated.

> Ministry descriptions help people get into the right positions and not get frustrated.

## IT GIVES A CLEAR PICTURE

Having ministry descriptions helps others see a clear picture of children's ministry, and it communicates that you believe the ministry is worthy enough to take time to have thought it through. People want to be a part of something that's significant. It doesn't matter if you need a new worship leader or someone to prepare snacks for the toddlers—take the time to develop a ministry description for each position.

The Bible describes the church as working parts of the human body. "The eye cannot say to the hand, 'I have no need of you;' nor again the head to the feet, 'I have no need of you'" (1 Corinthians 12:21). Every part of the body is important and so is every position in your ministry.

Let's go back to the baseball analogy for a minute. Some teams rely on a couple of power hitters, a reliable ace pitcher, and an overpowering bullpen. If you pay attention to good coaches, though, you'll notice that they build strength in each position. You can do the same thing.

# RECRUIT the PLAYERS

Recruiting the right players for your team will probably be the most challenging and time-consuming part of your ministry. Have you watched the game show *Minute to Win It*? In sixty seconds contestants can win big money! Unfortunately, some things in life take lots longer than sixty seconds—like recruiting volunteers. It takes time and work.

More than likely, new volunteers aren't lining up outside your office. If you wait for people to knock on your door or to respond to a plea in the bulletin, you'll probably be waiting a while. There comes a point when you need to make the big "ask," and asking comes in two parts.

## FIRST, ASK GOD

Start by praying that God will give you the needed volunteers. Sometimes we work way too hard at recruiting volunteers and end up with "volun-tears" because we can't get anyone to respond. "Volun-tears" are those who are willing to help but do it with tears in their eyes because they would rather get teeth pulled than work with kids. Volun-tears respond out of guilt.

Instead of having a team of volun-tears, wouldn't you rather have people who have been called by God? I have a question for you. Have you prayed about the positions you need to fill? Too often we come to the end of our rope and say, "All I can do now is pray." Prayer becomes the last resort instead of the first priority.

James puts it right where it belongs. He said, "You do not have, because you do not ask" (James 4:2). That's about as blunt as it gets. Jesus promised, "I will build my church" (Matthew 16:18). Ask God to help you recruit the needed team members to help build his church.

Early in my ministry I was pouting to a friend about the need we had for volunteers. He looked at me (I will never forget the look) and asked, "Have you prayed about it?" It was one of those duh! moments. He quoted, "Ask the Lord of the harvest, therefore, to send out workers into his harvest field" (Matthew 9:38, *NIV*). This young know-it-all learned an important lesson that day. Recruiting volunteers isn't my burden alone to carry.

## SECOND, ASK PEOPLE

Start by asking God, then start asking people. Let's say a guy named Nick thinks he'd like to volunteer in children's ministry. Surely he will find you after church, tackle you in the foyer, and beg you to let him serve. Right? Wrong! Why won't Nick ask you if he can get involved? The answer is probably one of these four reasons:

1. He's shy.
2. He doesn't know for sure what positions are available.
3. He has never worked with kids before and isn't sure he's qualified.
4. He assumes that you have enough volunteers and he isn't needed.

> The biggest problem? Your desk. You need to get away from it and start asking people to join the children's ministry team.

Right now there are people in your church who are using one of these excuses not to talk to you. Don't wait for them to find you. Get out of your office and start asking people to serve and be an important member of the children's ministry team.

Ask directors of children's ministries about the greatest roadblocks to getting new volunteers. Their answers might include that people are too busy, people's priorities are out of whack, the choir hoards everyone, kids bite, the senior pastor doesn't support the children's ministry from the pulpit, and blah, blah, blah. There may be an ounce of truth in those statements, but those aren't the biggest roadblocks to getting new volunteers. The biggest problem? Your desk. You need to get away from it and start asking people to join the children's ministry team.

God didn't sit back and wait for people to volunteer. How did he recruit his team? God used a burning bush to get Moses' attention. God used a violent storm and a big fish to convince Jonah to go to Nineveh and preach. God used a sycamore tree to help Zacchaeus meet Jesus. God used a blinding light to stop Saul in his tracks and get him to sign up for the right team. You don't have to use a burning bush or a big fish. But you do need to make the big "ask."

Dale Hudson is the director of children's ministries at Christ Fellowship in Palm Beach, Florida. He said, "Last year we added over six hundred new volunteers to our team. How? The majority were one-on-one invites by our staff and volunteers. Week in and week out. In my opinion, nothing is more effective than the personal ask."[14]

# Get the Equipment

Make sure team members have the basics. A baseball coach would never send the team out to play without gloves, bats, and balls. The team needs equipment!

When volunteers join the team, make sure they have the resources they need. This sounds very elementary, but make sure they have the basics like curriculum and supplies. Once they have the basics, encourage them to let you know what else they need. I've been consulting with a church that asked me to help them. They didn't know why their children's ministry volunteers were dropping like flies. In the first meeting with them, they told me that they didn't provide curriculum for any of their children's ministries and that teachers had to find their own materials. Guess what got changed first?

# SpenD Time TRAINING

Early in my ministry one Sunday morning, the phone rang right before I walked out the door of my home. Have I ever mentioned that I hate when my phone rings on Sunday mornings? You know why, don't you? On the phone was a Sunday school teacher who was sick. Doing what any young children's pastor would do, I drove to church and started looking for a victim—I mean volunteer. Anyone above the age of twelve with a pulse qualified. I found one such lady.

"Do you love kids?" I asked her. Of course her answer was yes. What else was she going to say? "No, Ryan, I hate kids!" To make a long story short, she became the sub that morning. It was probably the worst forty-five minutes of that lady's life. She failed miserably. Actually, I failed miserably. You see, just because she loved kids didn't mean she was qualified. Even if she was qualified, that didn't mean she was trained. I set her up to fail.

We'll talk more about training in chapter six. I understand the difficulties of training volunteers, but here's what I want you to understand. Team members need training because they are doing something important—very important! If they don't feel like what they are doing is important, they won't last for long. And even if they don't quit, they will probably grow apathetic and disconnected.

# PLAY BALL (AND SIt oN tHe BeNcH As NeeDeD)

Get your team members trained, and then let them play ball. I love walking around watching our volunteers in action. The hard work is recruiting and training. The fun part is watching volunteers do what God has called them

72

to do. Every weekend I walk through the church and watch some of the most creative people on the planet serve as children's ministry volunteers.

Part of keeping and developing volunteers is letting them have a chance to play ball. Sometimes as leaders we need to take the bench and let others have a swing at the bat. For example, a few months ago I decided to stop teaching kids' church every weekend and started letting other teachers be part of the rotation. Was I burnt out? Hardly. But it was time to give other people the opportunity to develop those skills. For too many years I've been holding tightly to the bat!

# Be THeIR BIGGest FAN

The best coaches are the best fans. Do whatever it takes to let your volunteers know that they are winners.

## GIVE THEM TIME

Not the magazine. Give them a few hours of your life. Find time to spend with your volunteers. Do lunch! I don't care what your schedule is like. Devote a minimum of five lunches a month to dining with your volunteers. Well, I guess it doesn't have to be lunch. Maybe it's an early morning coffee or evening dessert.

Do it! Put the book down. Schedule your first lunch (or coffee or dessert) right now. Right now! Trust me. This is important!

## GIVE THEM THANKS

Break the bank now and then and show your appreciation in a tangible way. I can hear it now: "But my budget is small." I get tired of hearing that excuse! Do whatever you need to do to find a few extra bucks and show volunteers how much they're appreciated.

People want to know that they're doing a good job and are valued. It doesn't have to cost a fortune, but don't get stingy and tightfisted with your money. Tokens of appreciation can be small, like a five-dollar gift card to Starbucks with a note that says, "Thanks a latte for all you do." (I stole that from someone.) Small acts of kindness will go a long way with the people you count on the most.

> Do whatever you need to do to find a few extra bucks and show volunteers how much they're appreciated.

## GIVE THEM BREAKS

Major league baseball teams play 162 games a season. That's a lot of games! However, the teams also take a break. Be willing to give your team a break now and then too.

Nick Blevins is a children's pastor in Baltimore, Maryland. Nick says, "A few years ago we created a summer team for children's ministry volunteers and we have great success with it each year. Anywhere from 30 to 60 percent of the people who serve on that team continue serving in the fall. I think people are more willing to sign up because they know the time frame (July and August), they know they don't have to serve every week, and they know we're having an orientation to help train them. Then, once they try, many of them continue serving. It's also a great way for us to give breaks to our regular volunteers."[15]

## GIVE THEM BRAGS

If you want more volunteers, brag on the ones you already have. Last year we started honoring a children's ministry volunteer of the month. Each month a volunteer is honored in the church bulletin, on a plaque in the church building, and he or she even gets to park in a special reserved parking spot. Get out the bullhorn and make your volunteers feel appreciated!

What are you waiting on coach? Sometimes we think recruiting and keeping volunteers for the long haul is rocket science. It's not! Put your team together and play ball!

**Interview with Deana Hayes**
Director of Children's Ministries
Light and Life Free Methodist Church
Indianapolis, Indiana

**RF:** I know that showing your volunteers they are appreciated is important to you. What are some practical ways that you do this?

**DH:** I like to remember days of the year that are special such as birthdays and anniversaries. I recognize their special days by sending cards or calling them. Occasionally, I also like to give them little sweet treats with notes of thanks attached. Oh, and my favorite way is a themed appreciation banquet that is held once a year.

**RF:** Everyone needs help recruiting volunteers. What are some successful strategies that you have discovered for getting the help you need?

**DH:** For me, it's keeping the vision before the people and communicating what our ministry to children is all about. We use different kinds of media to show the congregation how much fun it is to serve in children's ministry as well as keeping the vision before everyone. When recruiting, I use a direct and personal invitation that's fun and lively. And I remind people that serving in children's ministry has eternal rewards. It's all received positively.

**RF:** When you recruit new volunteers, what kind of commitment do you ask from them?

**DH:** I ask our volunteers to make a one-year commitment and to attend the quarterly training sessions.

**RF:** From your experience in children's ministry leadership, what are five deadly sins when recruiting volunteers and keeping them?

**DH:** Good question! Here you go.

1. No vision
2. No training
3. No follow up
4. No verbal appreciation
5. Wrong placement

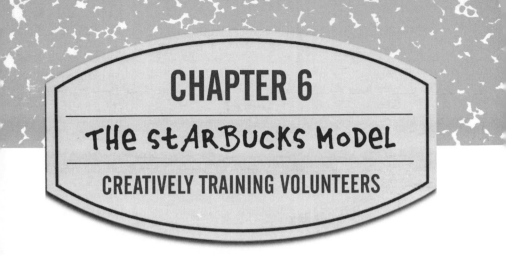

# CHAPTER 6

## THE STARBUCKS MODEL

### CREATIVELY TRAINING VOLUNTEERS

If I'm ever forced to get a part-time job (thanks for buying this book and narrowing the odds of that happening) I want to work at Starbucks. I've always thought it would be a cool place to work. Is it the coffee? No. Starbucks coffee has never been my favorite. It's the environment. Any student of the company knows that the employee experience matters at their stores. Any competitor can replicate the products they serve, but competitors can't replicate the people serving products to their customers. I believe it's people, not coffee, that makes Starbucks Starbucks.

Howard Schultz, Starbucks Chairman and CEO, says, "We built the Starbucks brand first with our people, not with consumers. . . . Because we believed the best way to meet and exceed the expectations of our customers was to hire and train great people, we invested in employees."[16]

Schultz says that Starbucks puts their employees first and their customers second. Starbucks knows that if they treat their employees well, their employees will, in turn, treat customers well.

If Starbucks puts so much attention into training and nurturing their employees (who have the job of serving hot beverages) shouldn't you do even more with the people who minister to children for the Lord Jesus Christ? After all, what's more important—a cup of coffee or a child's soul? The easy part is acknowledging the need for well-trained volunteers. The hard part is making it happen.

> The easy part is acknowledging the need for well-trained volunteers. The hard part is making it happen.

Approximately nine times out of nine (okay, maybe eight and a half out of nine) the biggest roadblock to training volunteers is time. Your volunteers are busy. So how do you train them?

In this chapter you'll meet five children's pastors who get it. They have developed customized training strategies for their ministries. They aren't stuck in yesterday's model of training. I think you'll enjoy hearing from them as much as I enjoyed interviewing them. Grab a cup of Starbucks and enjoy.

## Justyn Smith

Children's Pastor at The Church at South Las Vegas, Las Vegas, Nevada

The Church at South Las Vegas values volunteers, including their time. We call our volunteers "ministry partners" and there are a few levels of responsibility within our ministry partners. But no matter the level of responsibility, everyone values the time of our volunteers. For this reason our children's ministry has decided to make training as convenient as possible.

We have monthly meetings for our coaches. A coach is one level of leadership very important to our ministry. Coaches are very committed to the vision of what we're doing. Aside from that we have two big meetings a year that we ask all of our ministry partners to attend.

Why do we ask that most of our ministry partners only attend a couple meetings a year? They are extremely busy! We know our volunteers' time is precious. To compromise, we've made it easy to get and give information. We use "PJ's Friday Five" as a way to get out information. This is a five-minute video that we e-mail to our ministry partners and post on our Web site (thekidslv.com) and on iTunes®. This video reminds our ministry partners what's coming up and allows me to thank them and keep the vision in front of them.

We don't assume that everyone likes the same kind of communication. In other words, while some may like a phone call, others want a text, a Facebook message, or a tweet. For this reason we make sure we know how each ministry partner wants to be communicated to. I don't want to waste my time or our ministry partners' time if they aren't going to get the information. Another way we communicate is through our hidden Web site. This is where we post curriculum, schedules, etc.

We literally use any and all means possible to communicate with and train our ministry partners. This eliminates excuses and it works!

# ALLYSON EVANS

Next Generation Pastor at LifeChurch.tv, Edmond, Oklahoma

Ask yourself, "Can I squeeze in one more meeting, event, or gathering?" If you're like most people, the answer is no way! Shouldn't we assume that the same is true of all the amazing people who serve in kid's ministry?

Since we've discovered that there's not time to properly train new volunteers, should we just forget it? Or is there a way to equip and develop volunteers without scheduling yet another meeting of some kind? There are a couple of things we do that increase the personal connection that is so important when we do ministry together, without scheduling times to meet.

The first thing we do is self-paced online learning. If you search for that phrase online, you'll find several different amazing tools to use. You can create lessons to equip your group of volunteers that include an orientation, vision casting, and training. With this resource, a learner can sit in bed at 2:00 AM and complete all the online courses required to do safe and effective ministry. The lessons can be incredibly fun, interactive, and diverse. It's up to you. As you create the training, you can include video, artwork, text, music, voiceovers, pie charts, and more. As the administrator, you can track who has completed the lessons. Quizzes and tests can also be incorporated. This is a wonderful feature particularly if the content includes things like safety policies or other non-negotiable material.

The second thing we do is video training. Online learning is great, but the lessons take time to create. Occasionally we need to quickly communicate changes, vision, or an inspirational story to fuel our team. Thanks to the Internet, we're all very used to seeing under-produced, quick-shot videos that are engaging and effective. With the use of your computer and a web cam or video camera, you can instantly get out information with very little trouble. A benefit of this medium is that it's personal because your face can be on the screen. The children's ministry team can see the passion in your expression and in your tone.

> Although we continue to find innovative ways to train our team, it's more important to build relationships with them.

Feedback tells us that "brief" is the key word. The videos quickly become stale and ineffective if we send a four-minute video every week. Keeping the video to two minutes or less and only sending them when there is something important to communicate increases the views.

Although we continue to find innovative ways to train our team, it's more important to build relationships with them. Let the personal connection to your volunteers be the driving force in developing the ministry.

# ROB BRADBURY

Family Pastor at Planetshakers City Church, Melbourne, Australia

We need to think of new, innovative ways to train and equip our leaders by removing roadblocks. When we remove roadblocks we maintain our teams and build momentum. Here are four ways we keep our motors running at Planetshakers on a busy, busy freeway.

1. Weekly training sessions between services. These sessions last thirty minutes and are short, sharp, succinct, and significant. It sounds like a contradiction to suggest meeting weekly, but if it's brief, it works. Everyone is already at church so no extra travel is involved. Because we respect volunteers' time, we don't have meetings that aren't important. We also meet monthly for a discipleship meeting that features no housekeeping, but only ministering to individuals' needs. These have become a highlight on our leaders' calendars.

2. A weekly lunch for all volunteers helps us connect, do life together, and bond as a family. Again, this happens weekly since we're already there.

3. Leader's curriculum online. We place all of our leaders' notes and files for lessons and information online. Leaders can also access MP3 files of adult church services they might have missed. We place online messages from children's ministry conferences. We also have a mobile library with books and magazines available for volunteers to access on Sundays.

4. iPhone® app. Our leaders can check the upcoming week's lesson, notes, and videos on their phones which has proved to be a big way we have increased the speed in which leaders receive information. This has reduced the time that volunteers need to spend in training.

These are four ways we've responded to a trend change. I hope it helps you in what you do for Jesus.

# LYNN PAYNE

Children's Pastor at First Wesleyan Church, Tuscaloosa, Alabama

I know my volunteers' time is very valuable, so I'm very intentional about training. There are only two meetings a year that all volunteers are required to attend and those are in August before our fall kick off. We make it as easy as possible for volunteers to attend by providing dinner and childcare.

During these meetings I don't talk about items that can be better communicated on paper or through e-mails. These meetings are for leadership development, inspiration, encouragement, vision casting, in-depth training, team building, and fellowship. We go over the little details quickly (schedule, rules, etc.), and I give everyone a binder of our policies and detailed information that they can read on their own time. I send weekly e-mails with announcements and information, as well as encouragement and reaffirmation of our purpose and mission.

Once a month I meet with my core leadership team. This team consists of the key leaders of every area of the ministry. During this time I invest in them, love on them, and build solid relationships—which I've found is one of the best things I can do for my leaders. I also look for creative ways to help them grow and develop. I send them interesting articles, bring in consultants, and sometimes we visit other churches. I'm always looking for ways we can grow together as a team.

Training is more than just telling volunteers what to do. Training is passing on God's vision, sharing life together, and building up volunteers as leaders and individuals.

## ANNIe oostINg

Children's Pastor at Mars Hills Bible Church, Grandville, Michigan

I hired a personal trainer a year and a half ago. My trainer inspires me and models the correct movements so that even basic exercises give me optimal results. Having a trainer gives me a partner to hold me accountable and push me to excellence. In the same way my personal trainer has helped me be successful, our kid's ministry In-Service Training strategy equips a team of leadership volunteers to provide hands-on learning experiences for volunteers during the Sunday morning program. Because our volunteers consistently serve each Sunday, we know they won't miss the training as they might during the week.

> One month the training helps volunteers learn different ways of engaging kids in prayer.

By training volunteers during the service, they not only acquire tools, but they can immediately practice them with the kids. For instance, one month the training helps volunteers learn different ways of engaging kids in prayer. Since volunteers praying with first graders need different tips than those praying with fourth graders, a leadership volunteer will model age-appropriate prayer tools during an all-room activity. Then the leader encourages small-group leaders to apply what they just learned by doing a similar prayer activity with the kids in their small groups. The leadership volunteer can continue to coach the small group leaders throughout the year.

The issue of training volunteers on policies is also addressed on Sunday mornings. Rather than having volunteers read an entire binder of policies at the beginning of the year, we display policy cards in the physical place where the policies are to be implemented. This gives immediate and direct application that results in greater retention. To ensure that volunteers are reading the policies, we have them initial the policy cards when they read them. We also put short quizzes in their name tags that they hand in so they can be in the running for prizes.

In-Service Training goes beyond addressing the age-old problem of low attendance at weeknight training events. In-Service Training allows for intentional training with immediate hands-on application so that volunteers and kids alike are getting the most out of their Sunday morning experience.

## WHILe your wHeeLs Are spinning

Are your wheels spinning? Before you start the next chapter, let me tell you something you are not allowed to do. It's a rule and you have to promise that you'll keep it. Promise?

Here it is. Whatever you do, you are not allowed to copy any of these ideas and try to do the exact same things in your church. That never works. These five people don't work in the same town you do. They don't serve the same people.

Don't copy—create. Form a team. Order pizza. Ask some tough questions (see the next page). Invent your own training strategy.

**HELLO**
my name is

Your Team

Think and talk about the training that's happening (or not happening) in your children's ministry. Discuss these questions with your pastor or with a core group of leaders in your church.

1. What kinds of training do our children's ministry volunteers need? Here are a few ideas to get you thinking:

   - Dealing with discipline problems
   - Working with kids who have special needs
   - Leading kids in prayer
   - Making the most out of the curriculum
   - Working with specific ages of kids
   - Partnering with families

2. What are some creative ways that training can happen?

3. When can training happen?

4. Who can help develop and lead the training?

5. What's our first step?

6. What's the step after that?

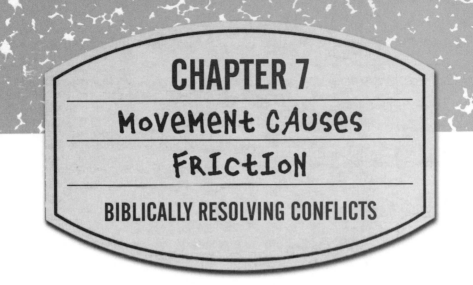

# CHAPTER 7
## Movement Causes Friction
### BIBLICALLY RESOLVING CONFLICTS

A man heard his daughter and some of her friends fighting in the back yard. He went out and disciplined her. "But Daddy," she protested, "we were just playing church." Ouch! Like it or not (and I don't), there will be clashes as long as the church is made up of people.

Dealing with sticky situations is never fun, especially if, as is most often the case, you think the other party is responsible for the stickiness. I never took a college class on handling conflicts between upset moms and nursery workers. A book never told me what to do when the church janitor is upset because of crayon scribbles on tables or when a parent complains to the senior pastor.

One day I plan to write a book called *Everything I Know About Conflict Resolution I Learned in Children's Ministry.* Problems are unavoidable.

Let's face it, when you work with kids, you have A LOT of movement (notice I capitalized the words A LOT). Where there's movement, there's going to be friction!

The gift of conflict resolution is not mine. I'm one of those guys who would rather run than fight. If you're a coward like me when it comes to conflict, this chapter is perfect for you. The next sentence is the chapter in a nutshell, so get ready to underline it. Great leaders are committed to resolving conflicts biblically.

## THe FINAL TICK

In case you have absolutely no idea what conflict is (which I doubt), let me define it. *Conflict* is "an open clash between two opposing groups or individuals." It can also be described as a "battle, a state of opposition, a disagreement, a dispute, or the final tick that brings an explosion."

As Christians, we don't need to turn to Dr. Phil to help us resolve conflicts. We need to go to God's Word. After all, it has a lot to say about conflict resolution.

*"That they may all be one"* (John 17:21).
*"Restore him in a spirit of gentleness"* (Galatians 6:1).
*"First be reconciled to your brother"* (Matthew 5:24).
*"Forgiving one another"* (Ephesians 4:32).
*"Speaking the truth in love"* (Ephesians 4:15).
*"Seek peace and pursue it"* (1 Peter 3:11).
*"Pursue what makes for peace and for mutual upbuilding"*
(Romans 14:19).

# Ten Battle-Tested Strategies for Dealing With Problems

From these and other principles in the Bible, allow me to coach you on how to deal with problems in ministry. How you deal with conflict speaks volumes about your leadership. Here are some pointers for dealing with problems when they come your way.

## 1. START ON YOUR KNEES

Prayer is the starting point when resolving conflicts. Ask God for wisdom and for the help that only he can give. Remember, Jesus faced conflict in his ministry, especially from within his own staff (aka the disciples). If he faced conflict, so can we! Don't let problems discourage you, distract you, defeat you, or depress you. Get God's help.

Prayer also changes the way you look at people. Nothing will change your attitude about a person more than praying for him or her. It's impossible to harbor bad feelings about someone you're praying for on a regular basis. You can't be mad at a volunteer when you're praying for her several times a day.

## 2. DON'T WAIT—DEAL WITH THE PROBLEM

There will be times when problems are simple and other times when they are severe enough to threaten your position at the church. Dealing with conflict takes a great deal of humility, resolve, and most importantly, a tremendous amount of wisdom. You've got to be committed to being a conflict-competent leader and taking action.

If you're anything like me, you'll be tempted to put off the problem for another day. Maybe it will go away on its own. Ever thought that? Ignoring problems only makes them get bigger. For example, if you ignore disgruntled volunteers, they may quit. If you ignore the concern of parents, they could potentially leave the church.

It's easier to control a spark than a fire. If you don't deal with problems when you hear about them, you may end up with a forest fire on your hands.

Here's one of the best ways to kill the fire. Take a breath, pick up the phone, and make a three-minute phone call to the person involved. You can call it "Ryan's three-minute rule." A three-minute phone call to someone who is upset (whether that person is in the right or wrong) can go a long way. In nine out of ten cases, the call will go much better than anticipated.

> Take a breath, pick up the phone, and make a three-minute phone call to the person involved.

## 3. PRACTICE EMPATHY

Plato said, "Be kind, for everyone you meet is fighting a hard battle."[17] The first time I read that I literally stopped to process it. Think about those words. Everyone you meet is fighting a battle.

Learn to empathize when a conflict is raging. There may be things going on under the surface that you don't know about. If a volunteer is wigging out over something ridiculous, he may be having problems with his teenage son or his boss may be putting too much work on him.

## 4. KNOW YOUR VOLUNTEERS

How well do you know the people serving in children's ministry? Knowing their strengths and weaknesses, how they work, what makes them tick, and what ticks them off will help you avoid problems before they ever come up. Let me give you an example.

I have a department director who requires over-communication. We work wonderfully together when I keep open the lines of communication. It gets rough when I stop talking.

Another department director doesn't require much communication but having lots of help is very important to her. If I forget to tell her about a change in plans it's no big deal, but I better make sure she always has enough volunteers! Good leaders know their people.

## 5. TALK TO SOMEONE YOU TRUST

The worst thing you can do is become isolated and try to handle things on your own. Find someone whom you can talk to who walks with God and has some common sense.

Talking to a neutral party is important for everyone. Too often we get caught in our emotions or we have a hard time seeing the bigger picture. While a neutral party can offer guidance, that doesn't mean that you need to talk to anyone and everyone who will listen!

Let me insert a small side note here. Keep the church leadership (especially your senior pastor) in the loop when there are conflicts. Your pastor doesn't need to know everything nor does he need to be involved in every detail. But it is important that he isn't caught by surprise. I hope you paid close attention in chapter three!

# 6. LEARN TO LISTEN!

This is tough. Even if the conflict doesn't directly involve you, it's hard not to form opinions from the beginning and make judgment calls. This week I was sitting in my office doing last minute prep for the weekend when in walked one of our church janitors. He threw some red flags that indicated a potential conflict.

Red flag #1: He didn't check with the receptionist and didn't knock on my door. He just walked right into my office.

Red flag #2: He bypassed the couch and sat down on the coffee table just a few feet from my desk.

Red flag #3: After my greeting the first words out of his mouth were, "Don't get mad at me for coming in here."

He went on to say that two tables were missing and he found out that I had borrowed them and not put them back. While he was venting, I dropped my defenses and listened. I could have said, "Do you know how busy I am? If all I had to worry about were two tables." Instead, I said that I would leave a note the next time I borrowed tables. (Let's hope that I keep my word.) I thanked him for talking to me.

Develop the skill of listening, hopefully better than the town sage in this story. Two men who lived in a small village got into a big argument that they couldn't resolve. So they talked to the town sage. The first man went to the sage's home and told his version of what happened. When he finished, the sage said, "You're absolutely right." The next night, the second man called on the sage and told his side of the story. The sage responded, "You're absolutely right." Afterward, the sage's wife called her husband on the carpet. "Those men told you two different stories and you told them they were ab-

solutely right. That's impossible—they can't both be absolutely right." The sage turned to his wife and said, "You're absolutely right."[18]

## 7. ASSUME THE BEST

Guard against jumping to wrong conclusions. Give people the benefit of the doubt. Relationships are hurt when you assume the worst of others. This is especially true when you hear that someone has said something negative about you. It's hard not to bristle up and get defensive.

Back to the church janitor and missing tables story. I gave him the benefit of the doubt. He wants to do his job and do it well. Part of his job is knowing where all the tables are. It's good stewardship.

When someone calls you on the phone to complain, assume that he or she has your best interest in mind. When your pastor calls you on the carpet about something he heard from a parent, assume that he is looking out for you and not out for blood.

## 8. ATTACK THE PROBLEM, NOT THE PERSON

An usher who gets mad because the kids are too loud loves Jesus like you do. A choir director who doesn't understand why you are

Deal with problems, but don't attack people. Assume that others have the right intentions just like you do.

taking his choir members to serve in children's ministry loves Jesus like you do. Deal with problems, but don't attack people. Assume that others have the right intentions just like you do.

There are very few things in life more harmful than attacking a person's character. Don't tell that usher, "If you loved kids more than yourself you wouldn't mind that they're loud." Don't tell the choir director, "You are the most selfish person in the history of this church."

Avoid "you" and "your" statements and replace them with "I" statements. For example: "I need help understanding why," or, "I heard that there was a problem in Sunday school yesterday. Can you tell me what happened?" Don't back people into a corner. Give the other person some wiggle room and don't put him or her on the defensive.

## 9. TALK YOUR WAY OUT OF A CONFLICT

I have found that 90 percent of conflicts stem from a lack of communication. The youth pastor didn't know you borrowed the ping-pong balls. The church secretary wasn't told that you expected her to collect the money and keep the records. The parents didn't know you were taking the kids outside. Sloppy communication is a breeding ground for problems.

A few years ago I took our fifth and sixth graders to an event at Cedarville University in Ohio. It was my first time taking a van full of kids out of state. It was a great event and God really worked in the lives of those kids. All was fine until Sunday morning when two parents cornered me. They didn't know that the kids would sleep in the dorms with college students, and they had a bone to pick with me. They thought that the chaperones from the church were staying with the kids. It was a communication breakdown. Everything would have been okay if the parents had known in advance.

## 10. CHOOSE YOUR BATTLES CAREFULLY

As the saying goes, don't worry about winning every battle—win the war. Let me share an example. Our church has a bus ministry. A few months ago I decided that the kids who ride our bus needed to come in and go out through a different exterior door. They had been using the entrance to our children's ministry center, but this was causing major traffic congestion when church dismissed.

The plans were made and we were ready to execute them. However, one of our leaders had a real problem with bringing those kids in through the door that I had proposed. Without going into details, she didn't think it was a good idea. She was okay with letting them use it to exit, just not letting them use it to enter. I disagreed with her but I chose not to fight the battle. But (and this is a big BUT), I won the war.

What was the goal? It was to free up traffic in the children's ministry center foyer after church. Did that happen? Yes. Learn to give and take.

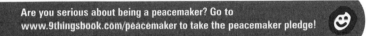

Are you serious about being a peacemaker? Go to www.9thingsbook.com/peacemaker to take the peacemaker pledge!

## Be A LIfeLong Peacemaker

Jesus said, "Blessed are the peacemakers" (Matthew 5:9). There is a special blessing for people willing to get in the middle of a conflict and bring peace.

Jesus also said that a house divided against itself cannot stand (Mark 3:25). Think about how houses are built. (No, I'm not a contractor or builder.) Load-bearing walls are extremely important. Without them, a house would collapse. I like being inside, but I don't want to be inside when that happens. Jesus was a carpenter. He knew that a house split down the middle would not stand for long.

Be a lifelong peacemaker. Helping people deal with conflict is not only important for you but for your entire ministry.

## Interview with Sam Luce
### Children's Pastor
Redeemer Church
Utica, New York

**RF:** How do you deal with parents in your ministry who are upset?

**SL:** I have found that most of the time when parents get upset it's because I haven't clearly communicated with them what is going on and what can be expected. When parents do get upset I usually try to listen to what they are saying, explain any areas where there may not be clarity, and always give parents options.

**RF:** Have you ever had to "fire" a volunteer? If so, how did you do it?

**SL:** I made many mistakes with volunteers when I was younger. I put people where we had a need rather than place them in areas where they were most passionate. In those early days I did have to fire a couple volunteers. In most cases I would talk with them and move them to another place in kids' ministry. But in some extreme cases I had to move them to another ministry. In recent years, when I have added new volunteers, I interviewed people to find out their areas of passion and place them on the team where they would add strength. The best way to avoid having to fire volunteers is to place them in the right place.

**RF:** How much do you include your senior pastor when there is conflict in your ministry?

**SL:** I am blessed to have an amazing relationship with my pastor and have been blessed to work at the same church for years, so I have a very good understanding of our church culture. Knowing the pastor and the church culture will determine when the senior pastor needs to be involved. As a kids' pastor, the better you know your pastor and the better you know the culture of your staff and church, the better you will be at involving the right players on the team at the right times.

**RF:** How has conflict helped you grow as a leader?

**SL:** One of the things that conflict has taught me is that people only understand in the ways they communicate to others. With people who are strong, you need to be strong. With people who are more laid back, you need to be more laid back.

**RF:** What is one word of advice you would give children's pastors the next time they experience conflict in their ministry?

**SL:** Embrace it. There is something about us Christians that we feel we must always love each other and never have conflict. We need to learn healthy ways to handle conflict in our lives and ministries, where we still love and respect each other. One of the reasons we don't grow as leaders and why our ministries don't grow is because we try to grow without conflict. Any life worth living, any cause worth living for, and any story worth telling, has conflict.

# CHAPTER 8

## WHAt's THAt HUM?

### THINKING ABOUT BUDGETS

Toys with missing parts. Chairs that are broken. Sound systems with annoying hums. Sound familiar?

Several years go I was invited to speak to a few hundred kids at a Christian school chapel. My arsenal was full of visuals including a PowerPoint presentation that I had worked hard on. While setting up, I asked about hooking my laptop into their video projector. The principal smirked and told me that if I wanted to try it I could, but the kids wouldn't be able to see it because the projector was so old. "It's been handed down," he said, "from the auditorium to the youth group and now to the children's ministry." I'll never forget what he said next. "That's how things go in the church, you know." Sad, but many times true.

More than likely you can relate to this story. I can. There is a mentality with many in the church that children's ministry gets the hand-me-downs because, after all, the adults and teens are more important.

Many children's ministries operate on a shoestring budget and on hand-me-downs. But what do you do when you have a vision that requires some big bucks? How do you raise money for your ministry beyond your budget? How can you stretch those budget dollars? Great questions! Let's tackle them in this chapter.

## THe stARtINg PoINt: ExceLLeNce

Getting the money that's needed for your children's ministry doesn't start with a spaghetti dinner, car wash, or candy sale. The answer is not found in fundraisers. Make a remarkable ministry the focus instead of making budget issues the focus.

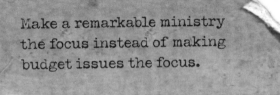

Make a remarkable ministry the focus instead of making budget issues the focus.

People get excited about putting money into a ministry that's excellent, that's going somewhere, and that's led by a person (or team of people) with passion and energy.

Don't be known as the person who's always crying for more or who blames everything on a lack of money. I've met people like this and I'm sure you have too. They will cry on your shoulder as long as you'll let them and complain about the money that they don't have. Listen, that doesn't work.

If your church's leadership has asked you to direct the children's ministry, they need to give you a budget to support that ministry. However (and this is a big however) you don't have to have all the money in the church coffers to make the ministry go somewhere. People are always amazed when they hear how small my budget is, especially knowing how many kids we minister to every week.

## THoughts on PLANNING your Budget

If you're new in ministry and planning a budget, or if you've been at it for years but need to take a fresh look, here are some thoughts to consider.

Keep the main thing the main thing. The main thing in your children's ministry is solid Bible-centered curriculum. Spend time researching the curriculum that best fits your ministry and is grounded in the Scripture. Put that first in your budget.

Don't just think in terms of a year but in terms of weeks and months. Take time to plan properly. Don't decide to budget one thousand dollars for curriculum unless you have calculated the weekly cost of curriculum and know that is what it's going to cost. If you put a bunch of big numbers on a spreadsheet for the year without thinking through your ministry year a week at a time, you'll probably find yourself broke before the end of the year.

Build flexibility into your budget. For example, you might budget five hundred dollars for an overnighter and not touch half of it. However, a month later you're two hundred dollars short on an appreciation event for your volunteers. Being flexible gives you some breathing room through the year.

Plan for income, not just expenses. My philosophy has always been that not everything in life is free, so why should children's ministry be any different? While I would never charge kids to come to Sunday school, I don't have a problem charging them for special trips and events.

Include projected income in your budget. For example, if an overnighter is going to cost two hundred dollars, include that in the budget. If you are planning on having fifty kids and charging them two dollars each, include the one hundred dollars of income in the budget as well.

Prioritize the money. Please don't spend half of your budget on flat screens, game systems, and toys within the first month of the budget year. You will end up falling way short and the important things, like curriculum and volunteer training and appreciation, will be in trouble.

Budget for new things. Every year when submitting a budget, I include at least one new big thing we'll be doing. Normally, it's three or four new things. This shows the senior pastor and the powers-that-be that the money is going into a ministry where exciting new things are happening.

Invest in more than kids. Will you attend a conference this year? What will you do for your volunteers? What about parents? Consider these (and more) as you put your budget together.

Include others along the way. Before submitting my budget proposal, I always run it by my senior pastor and my wife. Also, including other leaders in children's ministry and allowing them to give you honest feedback about your budget proposal will help as you prepare this important piece of your ministry.

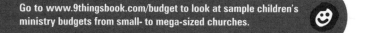

Go to www.9thingsbook.com/budget to look at sample children's ministry budgets from small- to mega-sized churches.

What do you do when you need money that's not in your budget? Let's say the Lord gives you a vision for a playground or leads you to start producing your own videos. Let's discuss that next.

# RAISING MONEY BEYOND YOUR BUDGET

Wouldn't it be nice if you could shake a money tree and money would just come falling down? It's not going to happen, is it? Sometimes you have to ask for money. There's nothing wrong with that. In fact, it can be an honorable thing. Paul often asked for money so he could take it back to the church in Jerusalem.

Sometimes God gives you a vision for something that's bigger than your budget. Here are three things to consider when you need to dig into the pockets of others.

## INCREASE AWARENESS ABOUT YOUR MINISTRY

Let people know what's happening in children's ministry. If no one knows what's happening, it will be hard to raise money. Here are a few ways to raise the flag for your children's ministry.

- o If possible, have a presence in the bulletin every weekend.
- o Include anything you can in the church newsletter.
- o Display flyers and posters on the walls of the church building.
- o Promote your ministries in the pre-service announcements in adult worship.
- o Get a strong presence on your church's Web site.
- o Use pictures and videos anywhere you can.
- o Let the children lead a church service.
- o Let kids share in adult worship how God is working in their lives.
- o Ask volunteers to share why they serve in children's ministry.

People will not give to children's ministry unless they know about it and believe in it. I get mail all the time from organizations wanting money. Whom do I send checks to? The ones I believe in the most.

## INVOLVE EVERYONE YOU CAN

The more you can get people involved, the more likely they will be to give to children's ministry. If someone has a connection and a level of personal involvement, they won't give five dollars, but fifty.

Want in on a secret? You have to remember that you heard it here first. Get as many senior citizens involved in children's ministry as possible. Why? Senior citizens have lots of time, love, and life experiences to share. And, many times they are the ones with money. Several dozen senior citizens are engaged every week in our children's ministry. They teach Sunday school, work in the nursery, serve as greeters, and are on a special prayer team that prays for the children, their families, and our volunteers every day of the week.

> People will not give to children's ministry unless they know about it and believe in it.

The likelihood of someone giving to a ministry that they are personally involved in is higher than you might imagine.

## INFORM ABOUT SPECIFIC NEEDS

The key word is *specific*. People want to know what they are giving to. The worst thing you can do is run a generic announcement in the bulletin saying that money is needed for camp. Not even a dime will trickle in. Instead, be specific. Let people know that they can sponsor a child wanting to go to camp for one hundred dollars or they can do a half-sponsorship for fifty dollars.

A few years ago one of our volunteers had a son in critical condition at a children's hospital an hour from her home. I caught wind that she and her husband couldn't afford to stay at the hotel by the hospital. I called fifteen children's ministry volunteers and asked each of them to give fifty dollars so we could take care of the hotel costs for a week. Within an hour, $750 was promised!

When you are specific, it gives people an opportunity to give. And be sure to spend money given for specific causes on those causes. Using that money for other things without explanation may cause people to not give in the future.

# st/Rt stretchINg

Not literally. Try stretching your budget dollars. Times are difficult and you need to find creative ways to make the most out of every buck your church entrusts you with. Here are a few pointers.

## GO WITH DOWNLOADS

Go online and download when you can. I got tired of buying an entire worship DVD for kids and only liking

### FIND GREAT CHILDREN'S MINISTRY DOWNLOADS

- www.worshiphousekids.com
- www.ministry-to-children.com
- www.kidzmatter.com
- www.kidology.org
- www.highvoltage-kids.com

one of the songs. Now I save money by downloading only the songs that we're going to use. Downloading music, games, curriculum, and videos will save you time and money.

## THINK FREE

There are a ton of free resources out there! All you have to do is start looking. For example, go to www.superstartpreteen.com for free parent e-newsletters, messy activities, and small-group activities. Check out www. heartshaper.com for free family pages, family e-letters, teacher training, and holiday and seasonal ideas.

Go to www.9thingsbook.com/freebies for a listing of all sixty freebies.

Andy Ervin led a workshop at Children's Pastors' Conference called "60 Freebies in 60 Minutes." Everyone in the room went wild for freebies! Here are a few he shared:

o D6Family.com: weekly e-mails that can be sent to parents with creative ways to keep the family spiritually linked
o Faithinkgames.com: children's Bible games
o PuppetResources.com: puppet scripts
o VisionaryParenting.com: monthly parenting e-newsletters, podcasts, and audio and video downloads
o Max7.org: children's ministry lessons and videos
o FreeCountdowns.net: countdown timers for children's ministry
o ChurchTechTalk.com: video shorts and graphic downloads

9 THINGS THEY DIDN'T TEACH ME IN COLLEGE ABOUT CHILDREN'S MINISTRY

## DO BREAK-EVEN EVENTS

If you want to have a family movie night, but there is little or no budget for it, do it as a break-even event. Make a realistic budget, set a goal of how many families will attend, and divide the numbers. Some of you may be having a hard time with this, so let me explain it this way.

If a family movie night is going to cost two hundred dollars by the time you get the movie and some popcorn, and you estimate that twenty families will be there, you need to charge ten dollars a family to break even. I figured that number in my head. (Am I good or what?) Break-even events don't cost anything out of your budget.

## ORGANIZE YOUR RESOURCES

Organization is the key concept here. There are people in your church who will never stand in front of a room full of kids or serve as small-group leaders, but they will organize all of your resources. Keeping supplies organized will help volunteers know what's available and you'll save money over time.

You won't have to buy new scissors every other week because you can't find them. You won't have to buy new beach balls every summer for camp because you'll know exactly where they are.

## SPLIT THE COST

If you're in need of a portable sound system to take to events like camp, see if the youth ministry budget will split the cost with the children's ministry budget. There's a chance that the youth ministry needs a portable sound system too. This concept can be your best friend!

## EVALUATE AND THEN EVALUATE SOME MORE

It's healthy every year to look at your programs and events to see what's working and what's not working. If you're pouring budget money into something that once worked but doesn't work any more, let it die. Put your budget monies into things that produce.

## WHAt'S REALLY IMPORtANt?

In closing, I want to remind you that more is not always better. Some churches have more money and some have less. Maybe yours has less. Remember that while some churches are financially poor, they may be spiritually rich. When it's all said and done, the most important things in life don't revolve around money.

One day Jesus will say to you, "I was hungry and you gave me food. I was thirsty and you gave me drink. . . . I was in prison and you came to me" (Matthew 25:35, 36). You may respond, "When did I do those things?"

Jesus might respond by saying, "When Ryder's parents were getting a divorce, you talked to him about his baseball team. When Lanie broke her arm, you asked about her cat." You might even hear, "You encouraged Laila to memorize John 3:16 and it made all the difference in her life!"

Jesus will explain, "As you did it to one of the least of these my brothers, you did it to me" (Matthew 25:40). Remember that it's not all about money. Relationships matter the most!

# Talking with Facebook Friends

**How have you responded when your vision was far bigger than your budget? Did you raise money, did you learn new money-saving tactics, or what?** Here is how some of my Facebook friends answered this question.

"I'm all about redos on a shoestring. You can get paint off an 'oops' cart for five dollars a gallon. Often you can find things that can be repurposed by going through your church's storage areas. Sometimes the greatest redo effect is actually just uncluttering (which is free). Recently I paid for a classroom make-over by selling some things on craigslist that we didn't want anymore." Julie Beader

"I write my own curriculum and save seven hundred dollars a year! I also first ask for needed items before purchasing them. We've had some great things donated!" Carmen Fleck

"Having money is only half the approach. If you need money for a vision, you need to form a plan, make a budget, and then PRAY. Approach investors and givers who share your passion and vision. If God is behind it, he will provide the funding. If he doesn't, it's your idea, not his. But be BOLD." Karl Bastian

"I pray a lot! God is our provider. He will freely give us all things (that line up with his will) if we will only ask." Tammie Jones

WHAt'S THAt HUM?

"One of the first things that I have done is to go to other staff members and indi-vidually ask them if they would be willing to contribute their talents to support the vision. What they bring to the table in terms of tech support, graphics, and volunteer support is something I could never put a price tag on." Tracy Parker

"This happens to us just about every time we have a project or big outreach event in the works. When we're certain God is in what we're doing, we plunge ahead, asking him to show himself big to us. He has provided every single time—often at the very last second, but he has always provided." Denise Grimes

"Visions should be bigger than we can afford and larger than we can possibly do under our own power. I would suggest you pray for discernment as to the validity of your vision and the next steps ahead. Proceed with these baby steps until your vision becomes more of a reality. This stuff takes time and if the vision is from God, the resources of time, money, materials, and people will come." Erick Ashley

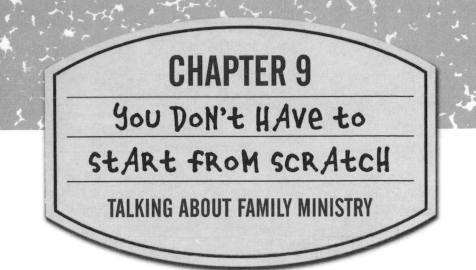

# CHAPTER 9
## You Don't Have to Start from Scratch
### TALKING ABOUT FAMILY MINISTRY

After graduating from college, I was hired as the first children's pastor at my church. My job description included things like teaching kid's church, overseeing Sunday school, and organizing events like Vacation Bible School and summer camp.

Today that job description has changed. It now includes equipping parents with opportunities and resources to be the primary spiritual leaders of their children (read Deuteronomy 6:1-9 to see the biblical foundation of this principle). It also includes creating environments where children, teens, and parents become thirsty for God (read Matthew 5:6). Whew! That's a mouthful!

The shift from children's ministry to family ministry is the biggest trend in children's ministry today. It has become the catchphrase of the

21st century church. However, it's more than a trend. It's an idea that's found in the pages of the Bible.

God designed the family to be the primary place where discipleship happens. The church's job is to come alongside families and teach them how to fulfill the commandment given in Deuteronomy 6:7: "Get them inside of you and then get them inside your children" *(The Message)*. It's critical that the church equip parents so they can be the primary spiritual leaders in the lives of their children.

When parents take the spiritual lead in the lives of their children, several things happen.

## FAMILIes Are PrepAreD

Do you remember the story Jesus told in Matthew 7:24-27 about the wise and foolish builders? Remember as a child singing, "The wise man built his house upon the rock"? One man built his house on solid ground—the rock. The other man built his house on shaky ground—the sand. The houses were built and then the storm came. Do you remember which man (and probably his family) endured the storm? The one on the solid foundation, right? This story is meant to be more than the lyrics to an old Sunday school song. There is a lesson for today's families.

Two families. Two foundations. One storm. Two very different results.

Both houses experienced a storm, but the one built on the firm foundation stayed standing. The other house had a mighty fall. We cannot make light of the importance of a solid biblical foundation in the home! If families are going to stay strong and endure the storms of life, they must lay a solid foundation by being intentional about spiritual matters.

# Young People Stick With Their Faith

I have yet to meet any Christian parents who hope that their children, as adults, will walk away from God. In the heart of all Christian parents is a desire for their children to be spiritual giants. However, it doesn't always end up that way. One of the biggest reasons is that parents often outsource the spiritual formation of their children to the church. It doesn't work! It takes a partnership between the church and home with mom and dad in the driver's seat.

The Bible provides no guaranteed formula for raising rock-solid kids. However, I believe that children who grow up in homes where parents are actively involved in their spiritual formation

> It takes a partnership between the church and home with mom and dad in the driver's seat.

have a better chance of sticking to their faith and the church as adults. Awana Clubs International recently released a study of Awana alumni.[19] This report revealed the important role that parents play in shaping the spiritual lives of their children. It begins, though, by sharing some troubling trends, including:

o   Over half of all church-going teens abandon their faith after high school.

o   As few as one in ten teens possess a biblical view of God and the world.

- Bible knowledge among college students has plummeted to all-time lows.
- The majority of children from Christian homes leave the church by the age of nineteen.

By contrast, most people who participated in Awana for six to ten years as children or teens continue to faithfully follow Jesus as adults. "Awana alumni enter adulthood prepared to walk with Christ for life," the report states. They were "found to be more devoted to God, His Word, and their local church, than even the nation's most committed churchgoers."

The survey results are clear as to why Awana alumni remain firm in their faith: "Consistent, long-term participation in Awana, accompanied by spiritual training from parents, reaps long-lasting results. When parents and churches work together to teach God's Word across kids' formative years, they produce young adults marked by steadfast biblical faith and character."

## God's Kingdom Grows Stronger

"I believe with all my heart that God is not calling the church to strengthen families for the sake of society," says *Children's Ministry Magazine* Executive Editor Christine Yount Jones, "or for the sake of simply building church attendance. Or even for the sake of the family itself. God is calling the church to strengthen families so the kingdom of God is strengthened."[20]

As you can see, the church/parent partnership is essential in today's church. Reggie Joiner, founder of the reThink Group and the Orange Conference, recently shared five facts you can't ignore.

1. Nothing is more important than someone's relationship with God.
2. No one has more potential to influence a child's relationship with God than a parent.
3. No one has more potential to influence the parents than the church.
4. The church's potential to influence a child dramatically increases when it partners with a parent.
5. The parent's potential to influence a child dramatically increases when that parent partners with the church.[21]

# WHAt Does FAMILy MINIStRy Look LIKe?

"Technically, anything that a ministry does for the family could be called family ministry," according to Reggie Joiner. "But that's actually part of the problem. . . . There is a difference between doing something *for* the family and doing something *with* the family. . . . Family ministry should not be another program you *add* to your list of programs. It should be the filter you use to create and evaluate what you do to influence children and teenagers. . . . If we really believe that nothing is more important than someone's relationship with God, it makes sense to combine the influences of the home and church."[22]

What are churches doing to partner with parents? It's not a simple answer! Because every church has a unique DNA, the way that your church ministers to families will be different than others. Some churches are changing curriculum. Others are creating a special church service just for families. Some offer classes for parents. The list could be fifty-eight feet long because family ministry looks different in every church. So how do you know what's right for you?

# DECIDINg WHAt's RIgHt foR yoUR CHURCH

You may already be doing family ministry in your church and don't even realize it. Or you might be walking down the road of deciding what that looks like for your church. Or you may be rethinking everything you do. The most important thing is to start or keep thinking about this and determine what's best for your church. Here are a few simple (or maybe not-so-simple) steps that will get you going or keep you going in the right direction.

## START WITH PRAYER

The first thing you'll be tempted to do is to find other churches that are effectively ministering to families and copy what they're doing. Please don't do that. It's great to find out what other churches are doing, but that's not the place to start.

Instead, start by talking with God about it. Don't go it alone. Get a prayer team together and ask God to show you what he wants to do in your church. After all, you work for him.

## LISTEN TO GOD FIRST, OTHERS SECOND

If you are serious about helping parents be the primary spiritual leaders in the lives of their children, you need a vision and plan that is supported by a solid biblical foundation. All opinions are welcome, but God's Word trumps them all. What does God want?

## ASK THE RIGHT QUESTIONS

You probably don't have five years to develop a plan for family ministry.

You need to get something going and soon. From the beginning, be smart with your time and ask the right questions, such as:

- o Who are the families in our church (two-parent families, single-parent families, blended families)?
- o What do our families need?
- o What is our church already doing in the area of family ministry? What's working and what's not working?
- o What are other churches doing?
- o What has worked in churches that are similar to ours?

## LOOK AT OPPORTUNITIES AND CHALLENGES

Take a good look at the opportunities and challenges that lie ahead. This is where you need a team.

Have you ever lost your keys and your spouse tells you that they've been right in front of you the whole time? (You were looking right at them but didn't see them.) Evaluating the strengths of your church, the opportunities that lie ahead, and the potential challenges are often difficult to see by yourself too. Get all hands on deck.

## FORM A WORKABLE STRATEGY

This is the most important step but it's also the most difficult. Since I'm learning just like you, I don't have a lot of advice to give you on this one. Remember the old saying that Rome wasn't built in a day? It's also true for family ministry.

So don't get discouraged if your ministry to families doesn't come together overnight. Take a good look at what you're already doing and start there. Add to it as you get the leadership and resources.

# A CLOSING RANT

One of the biggest things about family ministry that bugs me is people who think they have to change everything and start from scratch. Every time I go to a children's ministry conference people tell me about the new family ministry at their churches. I've heard:

- o We dropped VBS.
- o We quit Awana.
- o We aren't doing Sunday school anymore.
- o We started a family service.
- o I'm not the children's pastor anymore. I'm the family pastor.
- o We're using a new curriculum.
- o I'm so glad that someone is finally talking about family ministry.

Here's the question Beth and I have asked ourselves: Why does a church have to drop everything and start from scratch? Instead of reinventing every ministry in the church, take a look at existing ministries and use them to help moms and dads be the spiritual leaders they need to be.

> One of the biggest things about family ministry that bugs me is people who think they have to change everything and start from scratch.

That's what we've done at our church. We are creating new ministries and programs while at the same time using existing ministries to help parents raise godly kids. For example, we already have an exciting Awana program—so we're teaching parents how to make the most of it at home. We already have family worship on Sunday nights—so we're showing parents how to use Sunday nights to their advantage. You get the idea.

Whether it's the church/parent partnership, recruiting volunteers for the long haul, or getting along with your pastor and church leadership, I think we can agree that we all have a lot to learn. When I was ten years old, the movie *Back to the Future* hit the big screen. I remember watching it and being fascinated by the thought of being able to time travel. However, I've yet to find a flux capacitor that will take me to the past.

Nonetheless, we can all learn from those who have already been where we want to go. I trust that this book has encouraged you as you learn from my experiences and the experiences of others in children's ministry and identify lessons that will put your ministry ahead of the game.

HELLO
my name is

Larry Fowler

**Interview with Larry Fowler**
Executive Director of Global Training
Awana Clubs International

**RF:** Larry, I'm a big fan of your book, *Raising a Modern-Day Joseph* (David C. Cook, 2009). Can you summarize the book in a few sentences?

**LF:** We know research shows that when Christian young people leave home, too many also leave the church. The best solution, I believe, is getting parents to be the primary spiritual trainers of their children. Yet most lack a plan or even a vision of what that looks like. The story of Joseph from the Old Testament helps; it gives parents a biblical target as well as a plan for growing children who will follow God. My book unpacks the amazing parallels and contrasts between Joseph and the prodigal son of the New Testament. The book encourages parents to intentionally pursue the target of raising a modern-day Joseph.

**RF:** Most of the people reading this book really want to help parents raise spiritual champions. Do you have any advice for them?

**LF:** Wow—there could be so many responses. Let me mention three key things:

1. Don't let them off the hook. In other words, never stop talking about the fact that, biblically speaking, parents are responsible for the spiritual training of their children. In a loving, encouraging way, keep reminding them in every communication that you do.

2. Work on motivating parents. We do a pretty good job of making parents feel guilty, but what do we do to help them spiritually raise their kids? Use both extrinsic and intrinsic things to motivate—recognize, reward, celebrate, personally commend, and challenge. I believe this is the missing piece; the biblical pattern is clear, and there are certainly enough tools available.

3. Give them a target. Parents are so motivated when they have a target. Just let them hear that with more practice, their soccer player could be a star. Just watch them respond! I suggest adding intermediate targets, including what children should know and become at two- to four-year intervals throughout their growing up years. Celebrate with and honor parents who work with their children to reach those targets.

**RF:** What is the biggest word of advice you would give to a church that is thinking about family ministry and determining what's best for their church?

**LF:** Stay laser-focused on *changing culture*—not our societal culture, though that would be great—but *the culture of the Christian home*. Changing culture takes lots of time and it takes many influences from many sources.

# About the Author

Ryan Frank is passionate about children's ministry, particularly in helping others be successful in children's ministry.

Ryan and his wife, Beth, created KidzMatter Ministries in 2004 (www.kidzmatter.com). KidzMatter is a ministry that exists to help those who serve kids in the church. KidzMatter impacts thousands of churches through its online resources, curriculum (*The Kitchen*), and magazine (*K! Magazine)*. Ryan has served for fifteen years as the children's pastor at Liberty Baptist Church in Sweetser, Indiana.

He also serves on the board of directors for the International Network of Children's Ministry (providers of the Children's Pastors' Conference) and the American Children's Ministers' Association. Ryan graduated from Indiana Wesleyan University with a degree in Christian Education and holds a master's degree in Biblical Exposition.

Ryan and Beth reside in Converse, Indiana. Their two most important disciples are their beautiful daughters, Luci and Londyn. As a family, they enjoy traveling, water parks, and spending time with family and friends.

Ryan blogs at www.ryanfrank.com. You can also follow him on Twitter (twitter.com/r_frank).

# Notes

1. George Barna, *Transforming Children Into Spiritual Champions* (Ventura: Regal Books, 2003), 34.

2. Lilly Conforti, e-mail message to author, September 2, 2010.

3. The Barna Group, "Barna Survey Examines Changes in Worldview Among Christians over the Past 13 Years," March 6, 2009, http://www.barna.org/barna-update/article/21-transformation/252-barn...es-in-worldview-among-christians-over-the-past-13-years?q=worldview (accessed August 26, 2010).

4. http://pixar.wikia.com/Woody (accessed July 30, 2010).

5. Janet and Geoff Benge, *Gladys Aylward* (Seattle: YWAM Publishing, 1998), 19, 159, 171, 192.

6. Dr. Wess Stafford, *Too Small to Ignore* (Colorado Springs: WaterBrook Press, 2005), 11.

7. Lynda Freeman, "Thank You Notes," *Children's Ministry Magazine*, May–June 2003, http://www.childrensministry.com/backissues/detail.asp?ID=4830 (accessed August 28, 2010).

8. Janice Dickey, e-mail message to author, September 16, 2010.

9. Andy Ervin, comment on Ryan Frank, "Fighting Staff Infections — Part 3," Ryanfrank.com, http://www.ryanfrank.com/2009/08/fighting-staff-infections---part-3/ (accessed July 29, 2010).

10. Bill Hybels, "What Every Children's Ministry Leader Needs to Know," *Today's Children's Ministry*, March 8, 2005, http://www.christianitytoday.com/childrensministry/leadership/whateverychildrensleader.html (accessed September 2, 2010).

11. Daniel Sherman, "How to Pray for Your P-A-S-T-O-R," *My-Pastor.com*, http://www.my-pastor.com (accessed August 29, 2010).

12. Thomas Friedman, *The World Is Flat: A Brief History of the Twenty-first Century* (New York: Farrar, Straus and Giroux, 2005).

13. Information taken from Internet World Stats, December 31, 2009, http://www.internetworldstats.com/stats.htm (accessed June 30, 2010).

14. Dale Hudson, comment on Rob Livingston, "Recruiting Volunteers for Children's Ministry," *CMConnect.org*, May 25, 2010, http://cmconnect.ning.com/forum/topics/recruiting-volunteers-for (accessed July 29, 2010).

15. Nick Blevins, comment on Rob Livingston, "Recruiting Volunteers for Children's Ministry," *CMConnect.org*, May 25, 2010, http://cmconnect.ning.com/forum/topics/recruiting-volunteers-for (accessed July 29, 2010).

16. Howard Schultz and Dori Jones Yang, *Pour Your Heart Into It* (New York: Hyperion, 1997), 245.

17. Plato, http://www.brainyquote.com.

18. David Moore, "World Markets," *Vital Speeches of the Day*, May 1992, EBSCO Publishing, 684.

19. Information in this section was taken from "Awana Alumni Study," http://www3.awana.org/alumnistudy (accessed August 29, 2010).

20. Christine Yount Jones, "A Blueprint for Family Ministry," *Children's Ministry Magazine,* http://www.childrensministry.com/article.asp?ID=909 (accessed July 29, 2010).

21. Reggie Joiner, *Think Orange* (Colorado Springs: David C. Cook, 2009), 82.

22. Ibid., 83.

# Online Resources!

## ONLINE teacher resources!

- a quarterly newsletter teachers can modify to fit their ministry needs and then send to families
- holiday and seasonal ideas
- teacher training articles

## ONLINE family resources!

- family devotions (younger age levels) and parent devotional guides (older age levels) that correlate to the Bible lessons being learned
- ideas for bringing the Bible lessons home

www.heartshaper.com

## These new resources are in addition to all the special features already found in HeartShaper:

"Create in me a pure heart, O God" (Psalm 51:10).

"I will praise you, O LORD, with all my heart" (Psalm 9:1).

"I have hidden your word in my heart that I might not sin against you" (Psalm 119:11).

- Fun, focused Bible studies, Bible verses, and Bible skills that help children grow close to God's heart as they journey through the Bible
- Fun, multisensory activities that stimulate ultimate Bible-learning experiences
- Carefully developed lessons with relevant topics that address pertinent issues at the most appropriate times in a child's life
- Easy-to-use teacher guides with one lesson step per page, plenty of activity options from which to choose, and the special Quick Steps™ feature
- Complete teaching tools—audio/visuals that include an enhanced CD with music and printable files; student activity pages; take-home family resources

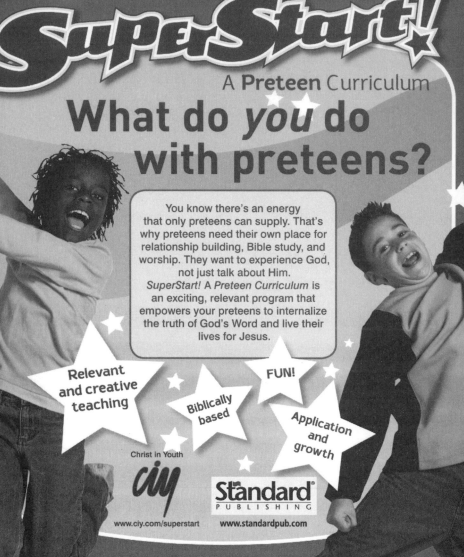